To,
Rachael

Lots of love
Shivanjali :)

'A groundbreaking book in many sense. You will not look at education the same way again. Very interesting for every learner. Equally interesting for teachers and parents.'

—*Sam Pitroda*
Holds 100 worldwide patents and is credited with laying the foundation of telecommunication and technology revolution in India

'*Fluid* has the power to transform the entire thinking and learning landscape with a single stroke.'

—*33voices*
Global conversation platform of business leaders and thinkers

'I think one of the misfortunes of Indian education is that it is not rooted in our own traditions. There are many scientific texts from ancient India, which have not been studied by us. Even the arts were studied by our ancestors through a mathematical and scientific perspective. An example of a perfect partnership of the arts and sciences. Ashish has taken an important step in addressing the problem of the lack of knowledge of our ancient texts through his book *Fluid*, based on knowledge gleaned from *Vishnudharmottaram Puranam*. His book is a must-read.'

—*Amish Tripathi*
Celebrated Indian author

'*Fluid* is a smart and well-researched book that easily crosses disciplines, in the search for a new understanding of learning and the mind. Rich in narrative detail and storytelling, it brings the reader forward and back in history in a way that inspires, instructs and delights. This book should be of great interest to anyone interested in developing a more "fluid" style.'

—*Rebecca Givens Rolland*
Tutor at Harvard Graduate School of Education

'A must-read before you set on the path of creating disrupting start-ups, path-breaking discoveries and next age inventions.'

—*Gaurav Jain*
Co-founder and managing partner, Afore Capital and Harvard Business School alumnus

'A stimulating introduction to another and different-and exciting-world of thinking and learning.'

—*David Palfreyman*
OBE, Fellow, New College, University of Oxford

'In a world where business models are getting disrupted everyday, Ashish argues very effectively that new managers need to be cultivated differently. *Fluid* describes this very aptly. A must-read!'

—*Nitish Jain*
President, SP Jain School of Global Management

'*Fluid* truly holds the key to a path-breaking mind currently locked behind the iron doors of formula education.'

—*Aman Iqbal*
Founder and managing partner, IQGEN and a PhD (Chemistry) from University of Oxford

'As a scientist in pursuit of solutions for sustainability and well-being of people and our planet, I recognise the immense need to work fluidly across disciplines by breaching traditional disciplinary boundaries. A powerful book and must-read for both specialists and specialists-in-making.'

—*Alark Saxena*
Director, Yale Himalaya Initiative and Research Scientist,
Yale University

'Fluid thinkers and an education system that encourages fluidity is the need of the day. This book written in a fluid style with 'fluid' illustrations is a great read to convince you of the need for a multidisciplinary approach to every aspect of life.'

—*Jeemol Unni*
Professor of Economics, Ahmedabad University

'The world we know is rapidly changing with technologies like AI, crypto and others. It's about time we relook at our century-old way of education and this book does exactly that.'

—*Vivek Jain*
Founder, CAclubindia.com and
LAWyersclubindia.com

'Adopting a fluid narration, *Fluid* brings to light the importance of flexibility, as opposed to rigidness, in one's approach towards success in any sphere of life. On a more direct perspective, being a professor in science and engineering myself, I totally agree that to do good, one needs to combine excellence in scientific concepts, fluid thinking in any direction beyond the concepts and a lot of artistic ideas.'

—*Amartya Mukhopadhyay*
Professor, IIT Bombay

'Every once in a while one reads a book that makes you think, question, and introspect. That book becomes a life-changing book. *Fluid* is a book like that. *Fluid* reminds us why success doesn't always come from following rules; sometimes we need to break and make new rules. If you liked Malcolm Gladwell's *Outliers*, you will absolutely love Ashish Jaiswal's *Fluid*. Exploring the themes of what it will take to succeed in the age of AI, *Fluid* is a must-read for every millennial (and non-millennial).'

—*Sulzhan Bali*
International development and global health specialist

'A breath of fresh air for every student, every parent, every trier, every risk-taker…everyone wanting to carve his own path.'

—*Jay Motwani*
CMD, TSD Corp

'I found *Fluid* to be a wonderful book with many visionary thoughts. *Fluid* explains very beautifully with examples how a flexible and open-minded person can do better in their personal and professional life and shape the society. The book touches many aspects including science, medicine, education, literature, artificial intelligence, relation between human and nature in a holistic manner. I believe this is the first book of this kind and is going to be most popular among our young minds.'

—*Ram Sagar Misra*
Associate Professor, Department of Chemistry,
Bananas Hindu University

'Like jazz, where its composition borrows from a variety of musical genres to combine into a unique art form, *Fluid* proves that moving to the syncopation of life instead of the usual downbeat rhythms of expected career trajectories has produced innovation's songbook for each generation.

'Applying the examples of da Vinci, Goethe, Jobs and others, as interdisciplinary masters, Jaiswal paints a portrait of genius much broader than the myopic confines of traditional definition. Readable, credulous, piquant and affirming to those who have found themselves tossed in a shifting marketplace, this title shows us that rare is the world-changer that is not also the skilled improvisor. Play to both your passions and strengths showcasing the aesthetic harmony of you is a strong message in this book. Jaiswal's must-read, transformative work will rouse you to applause and have you cheering, "Here's to survival of the fluid-ist!"'

—*Melvita Chisholm*
Global communicator and management strategist, Washington DC

'*Fluid* is a very forward-thinking book. It supports the idea that the boundaries we impose on knowledge are not pertinent anymore and builds on the many examples of fluid thinkers of the past.'

—*Mehdi Lazar*
Head of School, Ecole Bilingue de Berkeley, California

'A harbinger of a new commencement for millions of young Indians who find themselves unhappily straitjacketed into vocations chosen for them by society, family and peers. It is time you broke free!'

—*Harssh A Poddar*
IPS Officer and alumnus of University of Oxford

**Be more than
what you are taught to be**

fluid

The Approach Applied by
Geniuses Over Centuries

ASHISH JAISWAL

wisdom
tree

ISBN 978-81-8328-527-8

Published by
Wisdom Tree
4779/23, Ansari Road
Darya Ganj, New Delhi-110 002
Ph.: 011-23247966/67/68
wisdomtreebooks@gmail.com

Printed in India

Inspired by the fluid worlds of my beautiful daughters,
Navyasara and Nayantara

Contents

Let's Start With Malvina Reynolds   *xiii*

Anti-fluid

Artists Only Do Arts   3

Scientists Only Do Science   11

Businessmen Only Do Business   17

Anti-fluidity   29

Artists Doing Science   37

Scientists Doing Arts   55

Businessmen Doing Arts And Sciences   65

The Dangers Of Entering Machine Age With An Anti-fluid Mind

Our Lives And Careers From Hereon   83

The Ones Who Can Copy Better   85

Yogini, Shakespeare, Mimicking And Machines   93

Evolution Of A Rebellious Child   101

Lessons On Artificial Intelligence From
    A Nineteenth-century Storyteller   109

But, I Am A Specialist, My Friend

Like A Two-faced Snake, Our Two-faced Education   129
The Pain Of A World-class Specialist   133
The Sad Story Of A Brilliant Mind   141

The Fluid Specialists

'Be Water, My Friend'   149
The School That Produces The Highest Number Of
    Nobel Laureates   163

The Bigger Fluid Questions

What Can We Learn From The Richest Man In The World
    And The Boy Who Broke The IIT-IIM Mould   177
'I Am Sick Of This Country'   191
The Power Of Combined Fluidity   195
Let's End With Fatima Al-fihri   209

Acknowledgements   211
Notes And References   215
Image Credits   233

Let's Start With Malvina Reynolds

Little Boxes is a song written by Malvina Reynolds.[1] But Malvina did not start her life as a songwriter. Born in the year 1900, in San Francisco, California to immigrant parents, Malvina was one of the few women of the early twentieth century who had a PhD.

But we are told that PhDs are supposed to become professors. In her early career, Malvina worked as a social worker, ran a tailor's shop and even worked at a bomb factory.

But we are told that those who run a tailor shop cannot write songs.

In her early fifties, Malvina decided to attend University of California, Berkeley to study music theory.

But we are told that we cannot go to universities at the age of fifty.

Malvina started composing and singing songs in her late forties. Malvina wrote *Little Boxes* at the age of sixty-two.

But we are told that we have to give up on our dreams by the time we are sixty-two.

Malvina wrote on upholding rights of women, equality, against nuclear testing, protecting civil rights, stopping wars and many such themes. Malvina wrote more than 400 songs including *What Have They Done to the Rain* and *I Don't Mind Failing in This World*.

In her seventies, Malvina was doing around twenty concerts a year and against the advice of many, she continued to perform until shortly before her brief illness and death.

But Malvina was not the one who would act as per the perceptions and myths of the world. Malvina was more than what she was taught to be.

Malvina Reynolds was fluid.

I start by reproducing *Little Boxes* as homage to Malvina whose life is a true reflection of the spirit of this book.

LITTLE BOXES

Little boxes on the hillside,
Little boxes made of ticky tacky,
Little boxes on the hillside,
Little boxes all the same.
There's a green one and a pink one
And a blue one and a yellow one,
And they're all made out of ticky tacky,
And they all look just the same.

And the people in the houses
All went to the university,
Where they were put in boxes
And they came out all the same,
And there's doctors and lawyers,
And business executives,
And they're all made out of ticky tacky,
And they all look just the same.

And they all play on the golf course

And drink their martinis dry,
And they all have pretty children
And the children go to school,
And the children go to summer camp,
And then to the university
Where they are put in boxes
And they come out all the same.

And the boys go into business
And marry and raise a family
In boxes made of ticky tacky
And they all look just the same.
There's a green one and a pink one
And a blue one and a yellow one,
And they're all made out of ticky tacky
And they all look just the same.

From the song, *Little Boxes;* Words and music by Malvina Reynolds
Copyright 1962 Schroder Music Co. (ASCAP) Renewed 1990.

Anti-fluid

Artists Only Do Arts

'A mathematical mind? So, that's what you think I am. And perhaps, that's why I don't truly understand what love actually means?' Mrignayani expressed herself with a rather emotionless face while looking straight into the eyes of Rishi. She was taken aback by what Rishi had just called her, yet she had managed to hold back her tears. Mrignayani considered crying a sign of weakness and tried to remain calm in turbulent situations.

'No, I did not mean that,' Rishi replied tersely.

'I am sorry, Rishi, but these were your exact words: I am a mathematical mind. I am an engineer. I cannot fall in love. A calculative mind is what you really meant.'

'That is not what I meant. You are taking it the wrong way. I was just pointing out that you may understand what love is in a completely different manner.'

'Different to what?' Mrignayani was finding it hard to control her tears. 'Tell me, different to what?'

'It was just an angry outburst…' Rishi tried to justify his terminology but was cut short by Mrignayani. 'Before I leave, why don't you confess that your tweet about Ayn Rand and the hashtag #hyperlogical was directed at me?'

Rishi did not reply.

There could have been some truth in what Mrignayani was saying. It was just two days back when they were out for dinner celebrating their six months of relationship, when *The Fountainhead* became the topic of discussion.

'Don't tell me you have not read *The Fountainhead* by Ayn Rand?' Rishi said with a look of surprise while holding on to his characteristic smile. 'Every engineer must know about Howard Roark, the architect/protagonist of the novel who refuses to become a mere follower or the 'second-handers' as he calls them—those who simply copy and do not have the courage to produce original designs.' Rishi's brief got both of them talking and they spent their entire evening discussing various dimensions of Howard Roark's character.

Mrignayani was shocked when she read Rishi's tweet the very next morning:

'I wonder how many engineers know about Howard Roark! Left-brainers, are you able to see beyond numbers? Life is not mathematics. #hyperlogical #heartovermind #soulofanartist #aynrand #thefountainhead #leftbrainers #rightbrainers

'Why don't you just say that your tweet was directed at me?' Mrignayani repeated her question.

Rishi remained silent.

***

For artistic Rishi, the number-crunching, money-driven world always seemed to be at loggerheads. It all started during the final months of his school life, when he refused to go down the typical university entrance examinations path. Rishi had often regretted the fact that he was made to study maths and commerce at senior school and as a result wasn't able to bring single-minded focus to his creative calling. While his parents wanted him to become an engineer, Rishi had always secretly aspired to become a full-time film scriptwriter. His parents hardly objected to Rishi's active role in organising after-school writing events and poetry gigs, dismissing them as passing fads. But when his letter of admission from a relatively unknown university to pursue a degree in literature arrived, it was almost as if a bomb pierced the roof of his house. The distant uncles, the distant aunts and even the distant neighbours, they all got involved trying their level best to drag him into their, as he would put, logic-driven world.

It took some effort, but Rishi successfully managed to drown all the advisory pressure under his iPhone playlist, which was full of songs by The Ramones—the famous American punk rock band of the seventies.

It's Not My Place (in the 9 to 5 World) by The Ramones was his favourite, looped song.

With the powerful rebellious Ramones on Rishi's side, his parents had no option but to give in.

With no maths or commerce to obstruct him, Rishi graduated in literature with flying colours.

As planned, as soon as he finished his degree, Rishi headed for Mumbai to fulfil his dream of becoming a scriptwriter, and at the tender age of twenty-two, he was already knocking at the doors of prestigious Bollywood producers.

We all know that Mumbai is an expensive city and breaks in the film industry are not easy to come by. Thus, in order to pay his bills and support his dream, Rishi took a day job, in a small advertising firm as a content writer.

Although he liked his work to an extent, Rishi found it hard to interact with the sales team or the clients of the advertising firm.

For him, they were always only interested in numbers—the commercial aspects of business—and neither wanted nor attempted to understand the creative intricacies of his work. Whenever he attended such meetings, he always felt he was back in the company of his distant relatives and nosy neighbours, who would always put their mind over heart.

***

Today, Rishi was on top of the world. It was hard to believe that only yesterday he had a tiff with Anjali, a junior member of his firm's sales team, concerning his work.

Apparently, a prominent client was not happy with the copy of a print advertisement that Rishi had been designing for their firm, and he had asked Anjali to get it improved.

Anjali and Rishi were standing near the office water cooler when the discussion took an ugly turn. Anjali took the draft copy of the advertisement out of her folder; to the utter horror of Rishi, it was all marked in red.

'Who butchered my words?' Rishi's voice was a little raised.

'Well, I did! But, you see, it's only based on what the client wants,' Anjali became a little defensive.

'Anjali, I don't understand your world. Now, you don't try understanding mine,' Rishi replied while snapping the paper out of Anjali's hand. 'Just tell him, now I won't even change commas and full stops,' he said and started walking away.

'Don't be irrational. At least give me a logical reason that I can pass on to him,' Anjali's voice sounded irritated as she followed Rishi.

'Logic!' Rishi paused and turned and repeated with raised eyebrows. He declared after a momentary silence, 'Tell him to talk to The Ramones.'

'The Ramones? What?' Anjali was visibly confused.

'Anjali, it is a matter of feeling,' Rishi replied, stressing the word feeling as he smiled and pointed towards his heart.

'*Merry Christmas! I Don't Want to Fight Tonight*,' he reproduced the beginnings of another famous song by The Ramones as he turned his back again and waved the printout while walking straight towards the firm's cafeteria, leaving Anjali b ind in utter despair.

A day had passed, and Rishi was leisurely stretching his lunch hour by checking random stuff on Facebook when he stumbled upon the 'Spinning Dancer' test, which seemed to prove that Rishi was right about himself all along.

The 'Spinning Dancer' test demonstrated that Rishi was a right-brained person, confirming his passion for arts over maths or science or commerce. For those who haven't heard of this test, millions and millions of people to date have taken the 'Spinning Dancer' test on the internet to find out whether they are left-brained or right-brained. The spinning dancer in question is a simple animated silhouette of a dancer continuously but slowly spinning on her toes. If you are a right-brained person, you see the dancer spinning in clockwise direction, and if the dancer appears to spin in anti-clockwise direction, then you are a left-brained person.

The human brain is divided into two hemispheres, left and right, and the 'Spinning Dancer' test explained to Rishi the distinct functions carried out by the two hemispheres, elaborating that humans have a tendency to use one of their brains' hemispheres over the other.

Left-brained individuals are considered to be analytical, logical, rational and practical. They do well in mathematics, the physical sciences and subjects dealing with business and commerce.

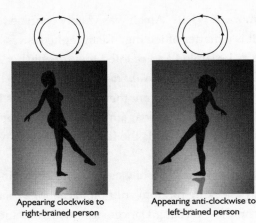

Appearing clockwise to right-brained person

Appearing anti-clockwise to left-brained person

The Spinning Dancer

Right-brained individuals, however, are creative people with strong imagination. Often termed impractical, such people are said to use their hearts rather than their minds, as for them, instinct is more important than logical assessment. Most world-famous writers, painters and musicians are said to be right-brained.

Suddenly, everything started making sense to the right-brained Rishi. He realised why he had never liked maths and why he always trusted his instincts over logic. Rishi now clearly understood why the world appeared to him as cutthroat, and why the left-brained Anjali might never understand his approach.

With this knowledge, Rishi's confidence was further reinforced. Although he now tried to be more sympathetic to those who brought analytical and logical arguments to his desk, Rishi knew that they saw the world differently.

The left–right brain theory had a profound effect on Rishi's life and choices—the kinds of books he read, the films he watched, the songs he listened to, the friends he made, the conversations he had, the people he admired, his Instagram subscriptions, his Twitter followings or the pages he liked on Facebook—they all became even more arts-centric.

***

Mrignayani was a software engineer who happened to stay in the same building in which Rishi lived. He developed an immediate liking towards Mrignayani. It was actually her name, which did the trick, as he had later confessed to her, 'Your name, whenever I hear it, takes me to the banks of a serene river where I am sitting on the steps of a small deserted place of worship humming a melodious tune.' Mrignayani's cheek went pink and she replied with a shy smile, 'I would have never thought that my name could do such a thing. All I keep hearing up to now is how long and difficult Mrignayani sounds.'

'Ha ha! You know I never thought that I would fall in love with an engineer but such is life.' Although those were early days in their relationship, Rishi had wasted no time in expressing his inner thoughts.

Mrignayani was not a confrontational type. She initially ignored Rishi's occasional remarks on how she was a mind-over-heart person but, as time went by, she would become nervous in Rishi's company.

Mrignayani had lost her father at an early age. Her mother struggled hard to keep their family afloat. With no financial backing, Mrignayani started taking private tuition when she was still in school and paid for her own education. Unlike Rishi, her life's struggles hardly allowed any time to read beyond her course books.

'I am not a philosophical person. For me two plus two is four,' she had once replied when Rishi was delivering a typical metaphysical sermon.

Rishi would often make Mrignayani notice her objective

analysis or rational assessment of situations and make her feel that she may not understand music, arts or literature in the same way that he did. Even her positive aspect where she avoided crying in adverse situations was seen by Rishi as a reflection of a person who wanted to control emotions with rationality. 'Let them flow,' he would often preach.

On their six-month anniversary night, Rishi gifted Mrignayani a book explaining the right–left brain theory and the importance of instinctive thinking.

'You remember that day you were telling me to be a little more organised, a little more objective? Just read this,' Rishi told Mrignayani and smiled as he handed over the book.

'Sure, I will,' Mrignayani had replied.

***

'Why can't you explain your tweet in simple words?' Mrignayani intervened with anger as Rishi started clarifying with an analogy.

The argument between her and Rishi became tense.

'Because that is not how emotions are expressed—in simple words. And I am not sure you can actually process when an emotion is expressed,' Rishi replied making no attempt to sugar-coat his feelings.

Mrignayani kept staring at Rishi as tears rolled down her che s. She collected her belongings and quietly left his room.

Scientists Only Do Science

'Latika is indeed beautiful, but I am not sure how much energy it will take to carry on such *nonversations* with her,' Chetanya whispered into the ears of Jaighosh with a smirk as soon as Latika had turned away. The trio had recently arrived in Oxford, England, from India, to study at one of the best universities in the world.

Chetanya had started a PhD in theoretical physics at Oxford. From securing an All India third rank in class X to scoring at the top in the IIT entrance exam, Chetanya had always been a brilliant science student. In fact, most of the people in his family, including his parents, had been reputed scientists.

Latika was a trained classical dancer with a Master's degree in Indian history. She had enrolled in Oxford's Department of Social Sciences to pursue a PhD in anthropology. Latika wanted to explore the relationship between the architecture of South Indian temples and the classical Indian dance form, Bharatanatyam.

It was during a monthly get-together of the Association of South Asian Students at the university that Chetanya gave his brutal appraisal of Latika.

In order to relive memories of India, members of the association had bought two cartons of Alphonso mangoes from the local Bangladeshi store. Chetanya, Jaighosh and a few other students had been standing in a corner, happily eating their mango slices and discussing the new Apple Park campus being built for Apple Inc. employees, when Latika joined them.

Hailed as Steve Jobs' final project,[1] Apple Park is the company's recently inaugurated headquarter campus in Silicon Valley, California. Spread over 175 acres[2] and standing four storeys high, Apple Park is designed in the shape of a flying saucer and appears to be a giant, parked spaceship when viewed from above. Apple Park has a curved glass elevation throughout, which gives this futuristic building the shape of a glass tube—similar to the tube of an automobile tyre. If there were a competition for largest circular glass tube structure in the world, Apple Park would win it hands down.

Apple Park: The flying-saucer-shaped recently opened headquarter of Apple Inc.

Jaighosh, who was from Oxford's Department of Computer Science, was telling this small group about the fascinating features of Apple Park, and his dream to work there once he graduates from Oxford, when Latika overheard them and requested to join in the discussion.

'I heard you guys discussing architecture, so I couldn't keep myself away,' Latika said, and introduced herself. She told the group about her interest areas and topic of her PhD, throwing in some facts about a relatively less famous temple in Mamallapuram (also Mahabalipuram), the Indian Ocean facing ancient town of Tamil Nadu.

Latika, however, did not share Jaighosh's impressed view on Apple Park. She expressed concern about the US$ 5 billion[3] (almost 33,000 crore INR) that was being spent on the campus, to house just 14,000 employees. 'With that kind of money, almost a million people from the poor countries of the world could be pulled out of poverty, permanently,' Latika spoke boldly, without any hesitation of a first meeting.

She even expressed her reservations about the design principles used in Apple Park: 'It certainly is breathtaking when viewed from above, but won't more people see Apple Park at ground level? Of course, you won't be taking the visitors on a helicopter ride to give them a bird's eye view before they enter the place!' Latika teased and questioned the group.

Chetanya, who was normally quite chipper, stood quietly listening to Latika. She hadn't noticed that she was the odd one out in the group, belonging to the 'non-science' camp as Chetanya frequently put it. Latika wasn't to know that— ironically similar to Apple Park's circular design—Chetanya had also drawn an invisible circle around himself for the kinds of people with whom he sought friendship. It was almost as though he had an inbuilt ranking mechanism that favoured people who exhibited an interest in select subjects. An interest in physics came right at the top, followed by mathematics and then chemistry. After that came the animal and plant sciences. Engineering barely made it inside his circle. Everything else, including the social sciences, was tossed into an imaginary dumping place he secretly carried in his head, named 'wannabe science camp'.

'That's not real science; that's indulgence! A way to pass time!' he would joke whenever social science came into discussion.

Chetanya strongly believed that the world—and education in particular—was ruined because of a lack of attention to real science. He often quoted VS Naipaul, the British Nobel Prize-winning writer, who had once said that he deeply regretted not studying the sciences at university. Naipaul, who graduated from Oxford with a degree in English, is known to have stated, 'I think I would probably even have been a better man if I had known or studied science profoundly.'[4]

'Better late than never,' Chetanya would joke, citing Naipaul, who had once also declared that universities should only teach science and technology, and ban all teaching of the arts and humanities.

Chetanya made sure to never share what he deemed 'frivolous' interests of an average mind—fashion trends, Bollywood, cricket, scandals, political news, etc.—on his Facebook or Twitter timeline.

In fact, he would not even share scientific news once he thought that it had caught the attention of the general public. For example, when the media had been going gaga over the Hadron Collider experiment to test the existence of the Higgs boson subatomic particle, Chetanya's Facebook timeline was silent. The floodgates opened when an acquaintance from the 'wannabe science camp' posted on his wall, 'Hey, what is your take on the God particle?' Finally driven to speak, Chetanya posted a lengthy reply, pointing to the ignorance of the general public, highlighting that they only remember science when it is fuelled by the media and continue to ignore the most important work that is happening endlessly and silently in laboratories.

His reply resulted in a Facebook mini-war between him and his friend, but, due to his command on the subject, Chetanya eventually emerged on top, and the non-science friend got tossed out of his Facebook friends' list as well.

'They don't understand how science actually happens, but they still go ahead and comment on it, just to show off!' he said to one of his lab mates a few days after the Facebook war.

When Latika commented on Apple Park and asked the group's opinion on what she had said, Jaighosh glanced at Chetanya and both exchanged smiles.

Chetanya, who otherwise would have just shrugged Latika off, spoke in a surprisingly mellow tone, 'That is an interesting observation about Apple Park. But such projects demand more complex analysis than a casual exchange. How about meeting later and discussing it in detail, perhaps over lunch?' Chetanya, who was smitten with Latika's beauty, presented his offer in a patient but undeniably condescending tone. Latika, who was unaware of Chetanya's strong reluctance to engage with non-science people on topics of his interest, also failed to catch his flirtatious undertone.

Anticipating an intellectually stimulating afternoon, she readily agreed to his offer.

Once the date and time had been decided upon, Chetanya abruptly sought to change the topic.

'I sometimes wonder what would have happened if Nikola Tesla had actualised his free energy device. I am sure you have heard of Tesla?' Chetanya addressed Latika, thereby changing the course of discussion.

Businessmen Only Do Business

'In that case, I will make sure that Pigeon stops flying, to immediate effect,' said Rahul as soon as Mr Sheshadri departed, and stormed out of the conference room, leaving Priya, Fatima and other team members in a state of shock.

Precisely when Latika, Chetanya and Jaighosh were eating their mangoes in Oxford, almost 8,000 kilometres away, in Bengaluru, India, a start-up named Pigeon was about to shut its doors forever.

Pigeon, which had been well on its way to becoming a full-fledged, home-grown technology company, aiming to manufacture mobiles for the global market, was now staring at a definitive death.

Pigeon had essentially been Rahul's idea.

Rahul had realised the importance of money ever since he was a child. His father was the third generation in a line of successful businessmen hailing from Indore—the business city of central India, also frequently called 'mini-Bombay' in business circles.

Although his ancestral business was exporting wheat, Rahul's father had diversified, acquiring a big government contract for mining sand from the banks of the Narmada River and becoming a partner in a business school. Thanks to these entrepreneurial instincts, Rahul's father had amassed a great deal of wealth.

And since Rahul's father had achieved all such success without having to use his formal education, he had little respect for degrees.

Although he himself owned a business school, he often laughed at the idea of business being taught in a classroom.

'I have twenty MBAs working under me, but they are all useless. I had to teach them everything from scratch. Some of them are even worse than my driver—at least he can process my instructions properly!' Panning those he called 'educated fools' was his most beloved topic at dinner time.

'How much will you earn after this?' was Rahul's father's favourite question to those studying at university. 'People like Bill Gates and Steve Jobs are not even graduates!' He would often give examples of those who dropped out of college and went on to make it big in life.

In Rahul's house, hardly anything outside of business was ever discussed at family gatherings. It was all about real estate prices, stock markets, success stories of the wealthiest business houses, the next big business idea, etc.

'Business runs in my blood—I can make money even out of nothing,' Rahul's father often said with a tinge of arrogance.

All this is what, in all likelihood, contributed to business running in Rahul's blood as well. Rahul chose the commerce stream after his X standard, and followed it with a bachelor's degree in business.

Rahul was a mediocre student as he paid little attention to his studies, but because most of his friends had plans to do an MBA, he wanted to follow suit.

'Clearly, you don't have to do it for a job, but if you really have to do an MBA then it is good to take it in a foreign country, for social prestige, if nothing else,' said Rahul's father, using his business acumen. So, rather than sending Rahul to do an MBA in India, which he reasoned would be within everyone's reach, he suggested applying for an international degree, which many Indian students couldn't afford to pursue.

Because of his low grades and lack of experience, it was clear that Rahul wouldn't be able to get into any of the top-ranked business schools. Besides, he didn't want to 'waste time' in preparing for the GMAT examinations. However, as in India, there are many business schools in the UK and the USA where practically anyone can get admission, as long as he or she is prepared to pay the required fee for enrolment. Rahul's father knew very well there were hundreds of education brokers who got large commissions from foreign colleges for sending students from India. He contacted one such broker from New Delhi and got Rahul into a London-based business school for a one-year MBA.

***

Before his plane had even touched down at Heathrow, Rahul already knew what he would gain from his course and the city of London. In addition to travelling for fun and partying with his MBA friends, Rahul spent most of his time exploring business opportunities, hardly enjoying anything else, like the art and science museums, historic monuments, exhibitions, theatre performances, etc. that the city had to offer.

Although one year is too short a time to change one's perspective about life, Rahul's stay in London did bring about some changes in his world view. For instance, now, instead of immediately working for his father, he decided that he wanted to launch a start-up, to which his father reluctantly agreed.

Rahul set upon the prospect for smartphone manufacturing in India, the fastest-growing mobile market in the world, having convinced himself that an inexpensive copy of the iPhone could make him a good deal of money.

With some pre-seed capital from his father, Rahul landed in Bengaluru—the start-up capital of India.

Rahul met Priya at a networking event in a cafe on Bengaluru's buzzing 100-Feet Road. Priya had a degree in engineering and computer science from a decent American university. Having worked in the USA for a few years, Priya was now back in India and was working as vice president in a start-up that designed mobile applications. Priya was looking to become an entrepreneur when she met Rahul.

Rahul's plan had been pretty straightforward: to create an ambitious feature list for a smartphone, write a compr ensive business plan for the company and attract the first round of venture funding.

Although Rahul had been convinced that he could bring his plan into fruition just by hiring a technical person, his initial year in Bengaluru had taught him that a tech start-up has higher chances of attracting venture funding if it has a technology expert to promote it.

Thus, the businessman Rahul convinced the engineer Priya to be co-founder of his start-up.

Fatima was Rahul and Priya's first employee. Fatima had a modest background. Her father worked as a lineman in the local office of the state electricity company and had spent his life's savings ensuring that his only child had a respectable education.

Fatima's father didn't have much idea about what career path she should pursue but, based on what he heard from his friends and read in the newspapers, a career in computers seemed to be the right choice.

Fatima did her bachelor's and master's degrees in computer science at a nearby college, and followed it up with a short course in an advanced programming language.

Fatima saw a job posting for a coder in Rahul and Priya's start-up on the display board of her computer centre and decided to apply. She polished her CV to prove that her life revolved around computers.

Fatima had a great sense of humour. She even claimed during her job interview, with a deadpan look, that if anybody were to visit her room, he or she would not see posters of film or sports stars but rather the world's top programmers. She also admitted that, if it weren't her first job interview, she would have attended in slippers and without combing her hair, as she had no interest in anything but computing.

Fatima got the job, but her reality was far from what she had communicated in her interview. She was an ardent fan of science fiction and her room was swarmed with DVDs and books of that genre. From *2001: A Space Odyssey* and the *Alien* franchise to *Guardians of the Galaxy*, Fatima had seen them all—multiple times. Coding for her was just a means to earn her livelihood, nothing more, nothing less. But science fiction was different. Her favourite pastime was alien spotting—Fatima spent hours on the internet, browsing video clips that 'proved' the arrival of alien spaceships on Earth, and deploring the fact that these clips were so often shot by cameramen with shaky hands!

Although the differences between Rahul and Priya started to show as soon as their office became operational, it was only in their first meeting with Mr Sheshadri that the seed of their future breakup was firmly sown.

Mr Sheshadri was a successful entrepreneur turned venture capitalist who had returned to India after a successful stint in Silicon Valley.

After returning from the USA, Mr Sheshadri did not choose to settle in Bengaluru but roughly 100 kilometres away, in his native village. A strong advocate of rural development, Mr Sheshadri soon turned his village into what he would call an *adarsh gram*.[1] All thanks to his contribution, his village had solar street lights, biogas-run kitchens, a sewerage treatment plant and a small hospital.

To keep his entrepreneurial instincts going, Mr Sheshadri also started a venture fund in Bengaluru, with a focus on telecommunications. Priya and Rahul met Mr Sheshadri at an event where budding entrepreneurs could meet with venture funders in person. Mr Sheshadri liked their sincerity and they soon started talking.

'What have you named your company?' Mr Sheshadri asked Rahul, and the young man mumbled a few names. Rahul hadn't been expecting Mr Sheshadri to take such deep interest in his venture.

However, problems arose when Mr Sheshadri turned his attention to Priya, 'And what about you, Priya? Do you have a name in mind?'

'Actually, yes. We could call it *Pigeon*,' Priya replied with a little hesitation, as she had already spoken about this with Rahul.

When Priya had come up with this name in one of their meetings, Rahul had simply shrugged it off.

'I am the businessman here,' he had said, barely hiding his annoyance.

'Just hear the logic b ind it,' Priya had insisted. 'Pigeons have a flawless sense of direction. It's like they have an inbuilt GPS, and by syncing it with the Earth's magnetic field they can fly for thousands of miles without ever deviating from their path.'

Priya had continued, pulling out a paper with a few sample sketches, 'Look, I have even got a few logo ideas.'

Rahul was really irritated by then. It was almost impossible for him to imagine that anyone other than him could brand his idea, let alone an engineer who had no background in business or branding.

'You know, Priya,' he said, 'business runs in my blood.' Rahul was starting to sound like his father. 'So you better leave the business decisions to me. The consumers are not going to be able to decipher this complex logic. Half of India's population is uneducated. Do you even realise that in my business plan I intend to sell my phone to even the *footpathwallah*s and *thelewallah*s? They won't even be able to pronounce the word pigeon properly!'

Rahul had shut Priya out back then with his business logic.

In contrast, Mr Sheshadri encouraged Priya to share her insight. 'What is your reasoning b ind calling it Pigeon?'

'Well, firstly, it is a commonly known bird,' began Priya, 'and secondly, as there is a huge network issue in India, we can tell our customers that Pigeon handsets have exclusive technology that helps them operate perfectly, even in a low-signal zone.' Priya once again explained the unique sense of direction that pigeons have, and how that attribute could reflect the unique selling point of their product.

Rahul was surprised that Priya hadn't discussed this line of thinking with him. Apparently, she was convinced that such information would be too complex for the non-technical Rahul.

'That sounds brilliant!' Mr Sheshadri latched onto Priya's idea before Rahul could intervene, 'I mean, it's a great name for a mobile phone company that doesn't depend on mobile towers for obtaining signals. This will also reduce the menace of mobile towers blotting the landscape. I am fighting tooth and nail to remove all the mobile towers from the area around my village. You know, there are a lot of coconut trees in my area; you would be shocked to know that since these towers went up, the coconuts have started shrinking in size. Imagine what they must be doing to human beings! If you can come up with such technology, I would definitely come on board.'

Rahul was a businessman, and although he was quite angry with Priya's out of turn suggestions, it was a big break to get Mr Sheshadri's support. Despite having no idea how they would develop such technology, Rahul was quick to twist his pitch, which now encompassed Priya's idea of mobile phones capable of operating even in low-signal zones.

And that is how Pigeon came into existence.

***

Mr Sheshadri kept his promise and agreed to invest US$ 1 million (roughly 7 crore INR) in Pigeon, to be put towards creating a workable prototype for Pigeon smartphones. Furthermore, he committed to funding further developments as and when these milestones were hit.

Although Rahul was initially reluctant, at Priya's insistence and Mr Sheshadri's approval, a substantial chunk of the funding was allocated to hiring more technical people to develop the prototype.

While Rahul was selling his success story, things at Pigeon were reaching a flashpoint.

As the technology required to develop a smartphone that would work even in low-signal zones was hard to accomplish, months passed by at Pigeon without success. Rahul was keen to come out with a prototype as quickly as possible, even if it was far from the desired stage of development, but Priya insisted on concentrating all of the company's resources and energy on research and development.

The differences between Rahul and Priya, which had been simmering for some time, were by now completely out in the open.

Mr Sheshadri had a fixed routine of meeting with the Pigeon team on the first day of every month. In the previous meeting, he had raised his concerns about the slow progress of development. Although Rahul assured him of a concrete result by their next meeting, Priya pushed to extend the deadline.

One day before their monthly meeting, Rahul bypassed Priya to give Fatima a few tasks directly. He wanted Fatima to search for open-source mobile platforms and vendors of hardware parts, so that they could come up with a concrete plan to realise a workable handset that would convince Mr Sheshadri that they were on the right track.

Fatima, who was working at Pigeon with no inherent passion, suddenly found herself in a situation where she was required to do something she really loved—exploring the unexplored. The task of researching an unfamiliar area made her feel almost as if she had been teleported inside a science-fiction story. Drawing on her talent for alien spotting, Fatima spent considerable time in probing the 'alien' territory of what the future for mobile phones would hold. She was fascinated to discover that a day would come when human beings would no longer require mobile handsets to communicate, as a chip with a call feature implanted in the human brain would simply do the job.

Fatima's investigative mind compelled her to go beyond the world of mobile phones and enter the world of holography.

Her imagination ran wild when she thought of all the things that the combination of mobile phones and holography could achieve in the future. For example, with the help of holography, in a video chat between two people, a person's hologram projection could create the effect that he or she is actually present in the room, unlike the current technology of video chatting in which the person is only visible through a screen. Further, Fatima thought of a classroom scenario, where with the help of holography, the students could actually feel that a remotely located leading authority on a subject is actually present with them in the same room.

Unlike other days when she continuously watched the clock for the day to be over, on that day Fatima was far too absorbed in her work to check the time.

In order to impress her bosses, Fatima stayed long past midnight to prepare a presentation on the future of mobile phones. She only went to bed after she had emailed the presentation to them—but even then, she couldn't sleep. Fatima was too excited by the possibility that her research would be a crucial factor in charting the direction in which the Pigeon would fly.

The next day, Fatima reached office and was shocked to find Priya and Rahul at loggerheads in the lobby.

'You don't even know how to spell technology, and yet you have the nerve to take charge of product development,' Priya retaliated, when Rahul told her that Pigeon would have been much farther ahead if he had just hired programmers instead of making Priya a co-founder.

'And how would you have done it? Through Ms Google?' Priya said, turning her rage towards Fatima when she saw her enter the building. 'Do you really think that some useless degree from a useless college makes you capable of directing a person like me?' Priya taunted Fatima in a humiliating tone. 'You cannot even *code* properly—but even that doesn't stop you from thinking that you can run the show around here.'

'You were never asked to waste the company's valuable resources on googling some nonsensical, lofty stuff!' It was now Rahul's turn to take out his anger on Fatima. 'If you had carried out my instructions properly, at least I would have something to show to Mr Sheshadri today. I regret the day I thought that I could do business with you techies,' he concluded and walked out of the lobby, leaving b ind a teary-eyed Fatima and fuming Priya.

Mr Sheshadri had always insisted on including all of Pigeon's team members in the monthly meetings, and so everyone was gathered in the conference room. He sensed the tension immediately and asked Priya and Rahul to explain. They each complained about the other not understanding the complexities involved in their respective roles and their contribution to taking Pigeon forward.

It came as a surprise to both of them when Mr Sheshadri turned his attention to Fatima and encouraged her to speak. Fatima hesitantly summarised her ordeal.

Nobody spoke for a while.

'Let's meet again tomorrow,' said Mr Sheshadri as he got up from his chair. 'In the meantime, why don't you guys discuss it and try to arrive at a consensus?'

The situation had unfortunately passed the point of any kind of compromise. Rahul asked Priya to apologise and when she refused, it was evident that Pigeon's short flight was about to come to an end.

Anti-fluidity
The wrong turn in our education

Whether it is artistic, scientific or commercial, the world seen by the primary characters of our previous stories is essentially the world as seen by them through the prism of their respective disciplines. Ironically, this disciplinary isolation—where we are not anymore interested to see beyond our own discipline—is essentially a result of the way we currently acquire education. Thus, the very education where we expect our myths and biases to be demolished is, in a way, contributing to building these very deficiencies.

Of course, the characters of Rishi, Chetanya, Rahul and Priya are fictional, but their subject-centric world view is certainly not a fairy tale.

In 1959, British scientist and novelist Charles Percy Snow (1905–1980) exposed the severity of the divide among disciplines in his seminal book, *The Two Cultures and the Scientific Revolution*,[1] in which he highlighted the wide gap between those studying and practising the sciences and the arts. Snow served the British government during World War II, handling the technical department. Because of the nature of his job, Snow had the chance to work with great scientists, as he duly notes[2]:

> I was privileged to have a ringside view of one of the most wonderful creative periods in all physics.

Snow continued to have this ringside view over the next thirty years. As Snow was also a novelist, there were days where he would both interact with scientists and spend his evenings with a circle of literary friends.

This fluid opportunity to intermingle with both circles gave Snow a unique perspective on how both sets had drifted apart. Snow writes:

> I felt I was moving among two groups—comparable in intelligence, identical in race, not grossly different in social origin, earning about the same incomes, who had almost ceased to communicate at all, who in intellectual, moral and psychological climate had so little in common...[3]

Snow observes that many of his literary friends expressed their ignorance when asked to explain the Second Law of Thermodynamics and, in the same vein, many of his scientist friends confirmed that they had never read Shakespeare. He concluded that a lack of exposure to the other academic circles results in both feeling hostile to and having a distorted image of the other, where:

- Non-scientists thought of scientists as 'brash and boastful and unaware of the human condition', and
- Scientists thought of non-scientists as 'totally lacking in foresight and unconcerned with their fellow men'.[4]

In 2009, Venkatraman Ramakrishnan, an Indian-origin structural biologist, won the Nobel Prize in Chemistry for the study of the structure and function of the ribosome.[5]

In one of his most recent interviews, Ramakrishnan expressed his concern that children were specialising too early in school. Making reference to Snow's work, he cautioned that the 'gap may have gotten worse'.[6]

However, not very many of us currently follow Ramakrishnan's advice of not isolating our disciplines too early. Our current education requires us to become masters of our disciplines—specialists,[7] as we commonly understand. Because of this, we not only need to choose our disciplines as early as in school, but if we are to become masters of our respective subjects, we have to give up on any activity, any learning that gets in the way.

But, had it been like this ever since?

In order to fully understand the warnings of Ramakrishnan and Snow, I decided to explore the progress of human knowledge. For example, how humans educated themselves when they started and how our modern disciplines evolved and were shaped over the centuries.

Although it is not possible to cover the compr ensive history of education here, I thought of a very simple analogy, presented below, which can shed light on how education as a subject was shaped over centuries.

***

If we look at roughly 2000–7000 years of evolution of how human beings have formally educated themselves, we can compare it with the continental drift theory.

According to this theory, Earth's landmass has gone through, and is continuing to go through, a process of change. For example, approximately 225 million years ago, Earth was a single tract of land surrounded by water. As a fun exercise, find yourself a large current world map and imagine yourself standing a few thousand kilometres south-west of South Africa, just above Antarctica. By virtue of sheer fortune, imagine that you have inherited infinite power, so much so that you can move continents! Now, pull all the continents towards you.

In this process, you would notice that when you pull India, you break it from the Himalaya.

The squashed landmass that results from this pulling will show how Earth looked approximately 225 million years ago. This unified landmass is termed a supercontinent, and is named Pangaea.

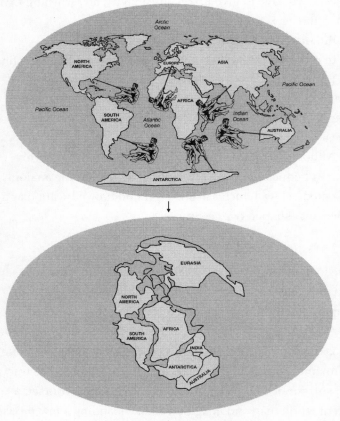

How Earth looked 225 million years ago

If you pull all the continents towards each other you will create Pangaea

Exactly like the unified landmass of Earth, the ancient scholars considered human knowledge to be an interconnected whole, freely exploring all possible disciplines.

For example, Aristotle (384–322 BC), a student of Plato and teacher of Alexander the Great, researched and wrote on the topics of zoology, botany, physics, philosophy, geology, poetry, theatre, music, physical fitness, linguistics and medicine, among others. Aristotle spent considerable time studying animal life, identifying and classifying over 500 species of fish, birds and mammals. In the field of physics, his calculations determining the spherical nature of Earth were beyond his time.

Coming back to the continental drift theory, the landmass of Earth is in a constant state of shift; hence, as soon as *Pangaea* was formed, the landmass started to drift apart. For example, the region that is today known as India moved northward until it hit the Eurasian landmass almost 50 million years ago. This collision created the Himalaya.

In future, as the Indian landmass continues to push against the Eurasian landmass, the Himalaya would continue to increase in height.

Similar to the drifting apart of Earth's continents, over the centuries, the disciplines, too, started drifting apart. Slowly, as time passed by, our education started becoming discipline-centric. The drifting of the disciplines continued with each passing day, and now they have almost become like independent islands separated by vast oceans. The students and practitioners of a particular subject remain firmly attached to their own disciplinary landmass.

As things stand today, the inhabitants of one island hardly mingle with the people of the other islands.

We are focused only on our own island—its trees, its grass, its landscape, in as minute detail as possible—and rarely bother about what is happening on the other landmasses. For example, a specialist doctor, such as a heart surgeon, hardly has time to know what is happening beyond his field—an investment banker may spend three quarters of his day dealing only with the financial world—a computer programmer may not ever look beyond the mountains of Silicon Valley.

This island-centric living defines the way the world appears to us. Having little understanding of what is happening on other islands, we only see the people, the culture, the issues, the progress and the opportunities of the other disciplines through our own prism of understanding.

Indeed, our reluctance to engage with an alternative understanding, our stubbornness, our biases, primarily stem from this island-centric education.

From our island, our discipline and our profession seem the most important ones for the world. Many a times, a majority of us remain busy learning ways to rise up the social ladder of our respective island to eventually emerge as winner among our fellow islanders. Our ignorance of the activity of other islands is often told with pride. We assume, perhaps, that the world functions because of our respective disciplines and hence we fiercely guard the boundaries thereof.

And when these boundaries get challenged, conflict occurs.

However, the progress of education also tells us that there have been people throughout human history who refused to jail themselves inside the boundaries of one or the other island. These people were curious to explore life beyond their islands. They built their own hypothetical boats and sailed in search of new knowledge. Because of this ability of theirs, I call them fluid thinkers. These were adventurers, unafraid to weather the stormy oceans, which existed in the form of threats and mockery from those who remained stuck with their existing learning.

These wanderers travelled from one island to another without a set path, without a map, without the fear of failure—learning freely, challenging existing world views and eventually changing the course of human history.

The educational journey of these wanderers inspires the idea of being fluid.

Artists Doing Science
From the curved bridge of Istanbul
to Tesla's inspiration

Before we go any further, let us address the anti-fluidity in the mind of Rishi—the artist.

Where we left off, the left–right brain theory had started to impact Rishi's life in a major way.

As unbelievable as it may sound to those who consider themselves left-brained or right-brained, the left–right brain theory with which Rishi had started to sculpt his life is complete nonsense, and the Spinning Dancer test is no more reliable than asking an octopus to predict the football World Cup winner.

In a recent interview, American astrophysicist and champion of popularising science, Neil deGrasse Tyson, rubbished the right-brain left-brain myth, stressing that trusting such fake divisions between science and art is taking our civilisation away from true learning. For those who haven't heard of him, Tyson is well known for unravelling the mysteries of the universe in a clear and concise manner, and has widely contributed to simplifying the complex disciplines of science for the layman. Tyson throws off the very fundamentals of this theory, which has propagated wrong notions about creativity:

> Don't call me left-brained, right-brained. Call me human…I am disappointed with some aspects of civilisation. One is our unending urge to bypass subtlety of character, thought and expression and just categorise people…you are either this or that. It is intellectually lazy. I am brained. Not left-brained or right-brained. *I have a brain [emphasis added]*.[1]

Indeed, we often discuss this right-brain left-brain junk as though people only possess one side! You would be amazed to learn how deeply this myth has penetrated our society. I have met dozens of people in my life who truly think that they can't be creative because they are hard-wired to be analytical, or they are poor in maths because they are right-brained!

I was almost shocked when I recently came across a *New York Times* bestseller (that I choose to not name) propagating this false theory. Broadly, the book concluded that, to date, left-brained people have dominated the world whereas in future, right-brained people would run the show! The book was based on the usual lame and fake division of people by the creative versus analytical divide.

Of course the brain has two hemispheres. Of course they may have different neurological functions. But to claim that one side loves science and the other does not is, to use Tyson's words, intellectually lazy. The left–right brain concept is nothing but a myth perpetuated by pseudo-psychologists of the internet era who fail to differentiate between fake and real research.

And to Rishi's disappointment, the Spinning Dancer animation has nothing to do with deciphering whether a person is predisposed to using the right or left hemisphere of their brain. It is only a clever optical illusion created in 2003 by Japanese designer Nobuyuki Kayahara,[2] for fun's sake and perhaps without realising that it would start getting used to propagate the left brain versus right brain myth.

When a student of arts believes that a good artist is not supposed to be interested in chemistry, physics, maths, markets or politics, or a student of science believes that a good scientist is not supposed to be taking an interest in music, singing or even dressing well, it is a result of not knowing that what makes us better scientists, artists or businessmen is going beyond the boundaries of these labels: being more than what we are taught to be.

To introduce you to the beauty of fluid theory, let me start by sharing with you the life journey of a fluid engineer who loved arts.

***

In 1499, the French King Louis XII attacked the Duchy of Milan. The Duchy of Milan was, at the time, one of the largest trade centres in Europe. In the fifteenth century, modern Italy was not a single country but one divided into various kingdoms, republics, duchies and states.

Because of this French attack, a talented and well-settled man working for the Duke of Milan suddenly found himself out of job. In search of work and in order to secure his life, this man journeyed to the nearby city of Venice to begin a new life as a military engineer. It was in Venice that he developed friendships with a handful of rich merchants from Constantinople (now known as Istanbul), the most populous and wealthiest city in the world belonging to the world's richest and strongest kingdom—the Ottoman Empire. The glorious stories of the richest empire tempted our able man to explore work opportunities in Constantinople.

The military engineer had been in Rome on a brief visit when he learned that the Sultan of the Ottoman Empire was in search of a capable architect for Constantinople's infrastructure.

Our enterprising friend wasted no time in writing to the Sultan. His letter included a proposal to design and build a giant bridge that no one in the world had ever thought of before.

Istanbul city's unique feature is the Golden Horn (the Haliç), a massive body of water that divides the city into two before flowing into the Sea of Marmara. In his letter, the engineer proposed to build an enormous bridge that crossed the Golden Horn.

It was for the first time in the world that anyone had proposed such a massive arched bridge. With approximately 366-metre length, 24-metre width and 40-metre height, this single-span (no supporting pillars) arched bridge was to be one of its kind. The engineer had used geometrical and structural engineering principles in the design that were exceptionally advanced for his time.

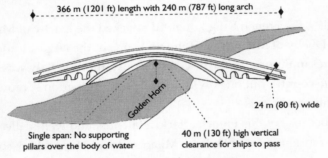

366 m (1201 ft) length with 240 m (787 ft) long arch

Golden Horn

24 m (80 ft) wide

Single span: No supporting pillars over the body of water

40 m (130 ft) high vertical clearance for ships to pass

Golden Horn Bridge design circa 1502

His letter to the Sultan read:

> I, your faithful servant, understand that it has been your intention to erect a bridge from Galata (Pera) to Stambul [sic]...across the Golden Horn ('Haliç'), but this has not been done because there were no experts available. I, your subject, have determined how to build the bridge. It will be a masonry bridge as high as a building, and even tall ships will be able to sail under it.[3]

The Sultan refused the proposal, fearing the bridge would fall due to the lack of supporting pillars. The bridge was never built, and the engineer's letter was confined to gathering dust along with the piles of other papers the empire deemed equally useless. Incidentally, the engineer never visited Constantinople (neither before designing the bridge nor after it).

For centuries the engineer's little notebook, which contained detailed drawings of the bridge, went largely unnoticed in one of the museums of Paris.[4]

In 2003, Norwegian artist Vebjørn Sand successfully built a 40-metre-long pedestrian bridge in Norway that was based entirely on the engineer's fifteenth-century design principles, proving that he had been correct all along.

When one reaches the end of the engineer's letter to the Sultan, it is impossible to disregard a minor detail: the name of this man who had once worked as a military engineer in Venice and who had designed a single-span bridge of such great dimensions in fifteenth century itself. The letter was signed:

Architect/Engineer Leonardo da Vinci

***

The above account of the architect-engineer Leonardo da Vinci may come as a surprise to many who only know him through Mona Lisa—unarguably the world's most talked-about painting.

Mona Lisa by architect/engineer Leonardo da Vinci

Unlike Rishi, Leonardo da Vinci had never been told that a brain could either be creative or logical, nor did he begin his career by analysing whether he was right-brained or left-brained. And thus, as his life's journey displays, he never differentiated between disciplinary areas and was interested in almost all aspects of creation.

While growing, da Vinci studied under a prominent teacher of mathematics, at the same time carrying out an apprenticeship in a painting and sculpting workshop, supposedly the finest in Florence. Beyond these pursuits, da Vinci also freely absorbed himself in wide-ranging subjects such as Latin, metallurgy, geometry, anatomy and aerodynamics.

Unlike current times, when a non-medico would never get close to a dissection table, Leonardo da Vinci not only carried out several dissections on human cadavers, but also used his background in anatomy, geometry and mathematics to study the human body in the most precise manner. The results of his fluid lens were mind-boggling. He created anatomical sketches with almost 3D scan precision,[5] which were so accurate that some can still be found in modern medical volumes.

Recently, the Royal Collection Trust, UK held an exhibition where the anatomical sketches of Leonardo da Vinci were displayed alongside the CT scan image of the same body part[6]— the remarkable similarity demonstrated the result of intersection of disciplines. It wouldn't have been possible without da Vinci's command over both arts and sciences.

Truly, the architect-engineer Leonardo da Vinci was the first person to draw several organs, such as the vertebral column and heart (with nerves, arteries and chambers), and even the human foetus (almost similar to a pregnancy scan), with photocopy precision.

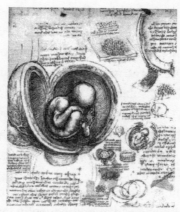

Leonardo da Vinci's notebook with precise drawings of
human foetus along with anatomical observations

Da Vinci's interest in aerodynamics helped him to study the
biomechanics of the human body—the science b ind skeletal
movements. He translated this interest to research the flight
of birds, and through that he was able to attempt to create a
machine that could fly.

Sadly, the subject-island forms of the current education
system distance an artist and a scientist[7] from each other. And
as they keep drifting away, they also take with themselves those
subjects they think belong to their respective camps.

Let us take the example of mathematics, which is now fully
owned by the science camp. And to this there seems to be hardly
any objection from the arts camp. We find evidence of this in
the segregation of subjects between the STEM and non-STEM
categories.

The word STEM was coined by combining the first letters of
four specific disciplines—science, technology, engineering and
mathematics. Although debate circling the division between
science and non-science subjects is quite common across
nations, the categorisation of subjects into STEM and non-STEM

happened in the USA around 2009. This was largely a result of concern expressed by the US Department of Education regarding students' lack of interest in science and technology. Barack Obama, then US president, announced a campaign to encourage students to pick STEM subjects.[8] Unfortunately, the increased attention on STEM subjects resulted in decreased attention on the non-STEM subjects—liberal arts, humanities, history, etc. Not only this, the categorisation reinforced the gulf between the science and non-science camps.

Of late, STEM has become one of the favourite words of politicians around the world, who frequently invoke it to steer the attention of students, educators, and the public at large towards themselves.

For example, recently, UK Education Secretary Nicky Morgan urged teenagers to steer clear of arts and humanities and focus only on STEM subjects:

> ...the subjects that keep young people's options open and unlock the door to all sorts of careers are the STEM subjects (science, technology, engineering and maths)...[9]

Her views perfectly match those of Matt Bevin, the governor of Kentucky, one of the states of the USA:

> If you're studying interpretive dance, God bless you, but there's not a lot of jobs right now in America looking for people with that as a skill set.[10]

Hearing the views of such seasoned politicians, we can hardly fault Chetanya, who carries that invisible circle that keeps non-STEM people out of his friends list.

Thankfully, there are many educators who strongly disagree with this faulty segregation and have been working towards dispelling the myth that a subject from the non-STEM side is not useful in mastering STEM-based industries.[11]

Leonardo da Vinci's intersection of his STEM and non-STEM sides helps us to dispel such myths.

Our Rishi may be happy to give away mathematics to the STEM camp, but the artist in da Vinci certainly would never have done this. He embraced mathematics, deploying it in sketching and aerodynamics with equal rigour, while famously declaring:

> Let no man who is not a mathematician read the elements of my work.[12]

Leonardo da Vinci, whose work ranges from drafting a master plan for the city of Milan to designing the first robot in recorded history, is an excellent case study for those who divide themselves into respective subject camps. Da Vinci would have refused to side with any. For example, in one of his letters to the Duke of Milan, da Vinci states as a proud STEM expert that he could produce eleven types of inventions, ranging from portable bridges to military tanks and armed carts. But he does not stop at that and proudly concludes the letter referring to his non-STEM skills:

> …also I can do in painting whatever needs to be done, as well as any other, be he who he may.[13]

Currently, many parents, children and even several schools tend to neglect physical training of a child in favour of academic work. For them, it may come as a surprise that da Vinci, who drew a detailed plan for a mechanised flying machine some 400 years before the Wright brothers,[14] devoted a considerable amount of time to physical fitness, so much so that it was said he could bend iron bars with his hands. Indeed, he was just as proud of this fact as he was of his fine art. And then, we often see intellectuals associating a certain degree of shallowness to things like fashionable clothes and makeup while proudly carrying out-of-fashion, worn-out clothing and dated hairstyle as a showcase of their intelligence.

The above painting is deliberately presented without a title so that we can all have a little fun exercise, at least for the ones who haven't seen it earlier. Try imagining who the person in the above painting can be.

Well, it will be difficult for many of us to imagine that the person depicted in the above figure holding a compass to a scroll is Isaac Newton (1642–1726/7)—one of the most influential scientists in the world. We all surely have heard the tale of how Newton got the inspiration for his theory of gravity when an apple fell from a tree and hit him on the head. My guess is, while recalling this story, many would perhaps imagine an aged, unfashionable and out of shape Newton instead of a six-pack, sculpted muscular Newton, the way he appears in William Blake's drawing.[15]

Such scholars who think dressing well is going to make them less of a scientist would be surprised to know that Leonardo da Vinci, one of the greatest brains on Earth, was quite particular about how he looked. Even in his old age, he designed and wore bright, colourful robes that were often worn by younger men at the time.

But fluidity was not unique to ones such as Leonardo da Vinci. Human civilisation has several examples of those individuals who refused to listen to the warnings of the world that crossing subject boundaries may belittle them as experts. In fact, contrary to the popular view, it was their very adventure of refusing to walk on a single path, that resulted in them creating masterpieces. This is exactly what happened with our next artist who faltered, failed and altered the course of his life many times, yet emerged as a winner in the end.

***

Born in Frankfurt, Germany in 1749, almost 200 years after Leonardo da Vinci, Johann Wolfgang von Goethe must have been a nervous wreck in the first stages of his professional life. After completing his law degree, he opened a small practice in Frankfurt at the young age of twenty-two (incidentally, exactly at the same age when Rishi reached Mumbai to enter the glamorous world of Bollywood).

We will never know Rishi's fate, but Goethe lost all his early cases and was even reprimanded by the judges for being too aggressive in his arguments.

His failures ensured that Goethe was in dire need of a career switch.

But if Goethe lived in current times—when students are forced to choose their disciplines before they are even aware of what kind of career path they wish to follow—he might not have much scope for a career change: the current education system would have already compelled him to leave aside every subject that wouldn't have helped him to clear law related exams.

Thankfully, during his school years, Goethe also leaned towards arts and spent considerable time reading. However, unlike many from the current generation, who restrict themselves to reading one particular genre, Goethe did not stop himself at only popular literature, but also delved into philosophy, history, theology and even texts from far-off countries such as India.

In Goethe's own words:

> …if the medley of fable and history, mythology and religion, threatened to bewilder me, I readily fled to those oriental regions, plunged into the first books of Moses, and there, amid the scattered shepherd tribes, found myself at once in the greatest solitude and the greatest society.[16]

The nature of my work allows me to visit several countries where I get the opportunity to interact with a huge number of children. A fact that has often worried me is the commonality in the list of favourite authors among these children of various nationalities. Names like JK Rowling, JRR Tolkien and Rick Riordan, etc. keep popping up. But then if we all keep reading the same, will we all not start thinking alike? I was thrilled when, during one of my interactions in a school in Sharjah, a little girl mentioned that her favourite read was an Arabic book on the life of legendry Hypatia—a fourth-century female mathematician who displayed exceptional command over astronomy and philosophy. Taking inspiration from the life of Hypatia, the little girl wanted to go into the field of space science.

As this little girl, Goethe was particularly mesmerised by the translated works of a famous Sanskrit drama, the *Abhigyan Shakuntalam*.[17]

Abhigyan Shakuntalam was composed by legendary playwright and poet Kalidas (addressed as *Mahakavi*[18] Kalidas), who lived in India at the same time when the likes of Pythagoras, Socrates and Plato lived in ancient Greece.[19] Kalidas based the play on the popular romance of King Dushyant and his love Shakuntala, as narrated in the epic text, the Mahabharata.

I am unsure if it is still the case in India today, but the tale of Shakuntala was a popular children's bedtime story when I was growing up. I still remember my grandmother tucking me up in a blanket, reciting the story to me.

Shakuntala is the beautiful daughter of a sage who lives in the forests outside the ancient city of Hastinapur (the city that later bore witness to all the events of the Mahabharata). On one of his hunting trips, King Dushyant, the ruler of Hastinapur, ventures into Shakuntala's forest and falls in love with her at first sight. They marry in a secret ceremony, and before leaving, King Dushyant gifts his insignia ring to Shakuntala, promising to return.

As days pass, Shakuntala becomes unmindful of her surroundings, completely absorbed in fantasies about her future with the king. In a tragic turn of events, she fails to accord a proper welcome to a visiting sage, who as a result places a curse on her. The curse dictates that King Dushyant will lose all memory of Shakuntala and will never return to the forest.

Shakuntala, now the mother of a teenage son, decides to visit King Dushyant, but drops his insignia ring in a river while travelling to the kingdom. King Dushyant fails to recognise Shakuntala, and he orders that she and her son be thrown out of his palace.

Several years later, a fisherman finds the royal ring inside the belly of a fish and returns it to the king in anticipation of a reward. As soon as King Dushyant sees this ring, he recalls his meeting with Shakuntala and immediately leaves for the forest to bring her home.

The son of King Dushyant and Shakuntala, who was named Bharat, became one of the most powerful kings in ancient India. Incidentally, it is after the name of Shakuntala's son that India is known as Bharat in Hindi.

It was between the future descendants of Bharat that the epic war at Kurukshetra, the climax of the Mahabharata, takes place.

Although I had heard this story many times, every time my grandmother inched towards the episode of the recovery of the ring from the belly of a fish, my young mind was amazed by the coincidence of finding that one fish among thousands of others.

Goethe's exposure to varied literature such as *Abhigyan Shakuntalam* rescued his dwindling professional life and, at the age of twenty-five, he produced what might be considered the world's first bestseller—*The Sorrows of Young Werther*, the tragic novel about an ill-fated love triangle.

In the novel, a young artist named Werther falls in love with Charlotte, a girl already engaged to be married to Albert. *The Sorrows of Young Werther* came to be a literary sensation in Europe. Just as the film stars of today, the novel's characters also became iconic. People started to dress the way Werther and Charlotte did in the novel. Souvenirs and other mass-produced items, such as crockery bearing imprints of scenes from the novel, were widely distributed, as per demand. Even a perfume, Eau de Werther, was produced to encapsulate the popularity of the character created by Goethe.

This craze, which the world was witnessing perhaps for the first time, was given the appellation 'Werther fever'. Indeed, use of the word fever with an event to denote popularity (as is so often the case with sporting events, such as 'football fever') only started after this incident.

Goethe's novel was so popular that Napoleon Bonaparte is said to have read it at least seven times.

It is said that Werther's tragic suicide in the novel caused hundreds of young readers, both men and women, to mourn for we s, and many committed suicide themselves, copying Werther's method of shooting himself. The term 'copycat suicide' was coined shortly afterward. The influence of the novel was considered so grave that it was banned in Italy and Denmark for several years.

Goethe went on to write iconic plays, poems, prose and non-fiction. His words inspired many other great legends: Mozart loved Goethe's compositions; Beethoven hero-worshiped him; in the Disney blockbuster *Fantasia*, the famous segment 'The Sorcerer's Apprentice' is based on Goethe's poem of the same name.

Goethe also wrote some incredibly quotable lines. The British Empire might have been encouraged to be less deceitful in their treatment of India had they followed Goethe's words:

> Divide and rule, the politician cries; Unite and lead, is watchword of the wise.[20]

Even the famous British rock band *Coldplay*, who—even in this age of the internet—manage to draw millions from their homes every time they play, would be jealous of the celebrity status that was enjoyed by Goethe some 350 years ago and many of us would be proud to achieve even a fraction of what Goethe did. But these accolades and adulations may still not have satisfied our beloved friend Chetanya, nor have him consider Goethe a friend. After all, what Goethe did belonged only in Chetanya's imaginary rubbish bin for the arts!

Perhaps Goethe had anticipated that his achievements as a writer would not impress scientists such as Chetanya, and hence our Goethe decided to try his hands at 'real' science.

***

At a time when people were rushing to the cities and deserting villages, Goethe, shortly after the success of his first novel, left the city of Frankfurt to settle in a small town. He famously declared:

I exchange the stuffiness of the town and study for the pure atmosphere of country, forest and garden.[21]

Impressed by his writing, the Duke[22] had gifted Goethe a garden in the countryside. In current pressures of education, we may consider activities such as gardening a waste of time and unlikely to contribute in any way to our learning. After all, no university entrance exam gives extra points to a gardener! But Goethe's time as a gardener was to change the course of science.

Goethe spent a great deal of time in his garden, and he soon fell in love with caring for his plants. To understand the differences between them, he spent hours observing and collecting hundreds of varieties of plant specimens.

Goethe had no formal background in botany; he learned it all by himself.

And after ten years of effort, the literary writer Goethe broke new ground in a field of science. He single-handedly developed the field of morphology, the branch of biology that deals with the study of the forms and structure of plants and animals.

The term morphology itself was coined by Goethe.[23]

Recently, together with friends and family, I took a countrywide tour of Italy. When we reached its southern tip, I was pleasantly surprised to see our very own sturdy Indian *kaner*[24] in full bloom, planted alongside Italy's dark pink bougainvillea. The lemon trees, with lemons the size of apples, almost looked as though they had emerged from a fairy tale!

Like us, Goethe was also struck by the diverse beauty of the southern Italian landscape—it was in one of its gardens that he conceptualised the idea of plant metamorphosis. In his groundbreaking work, *Metamorphosis of Plants,* written fifteen years after his popular novel, Goethe described metamorphosis as being the continuous transformation of living organisms.

Goethe proposed that if living organisms are continuously evolving, then they must all have a common ancestry. This is called homology. For example, our human limbs, the wings of a bat and the front flippers of a whale are all derived from the same ancestral structure.

Goethe's idea of common ancestry also inspired the stalwart biologist Charles Darwin to propose his theory of evolution. In a fitting tribute, Darwin mentions Goethe's contribution in his iconic book *On the Origin of Species* (1859).[25] I wonder how many artists of today can find their names mentioned in books of such scientific magnitude?

Incidentally, in true Goethean spirit, after writing a scientific book on metamorphosis at the age of forty-one, Goethe then wrote a beautiful poem of the same name in the following year, giving the process of transformation a poetic flair. Both the scientific book and the poem are excellent examples of how Goethe never believed in boxing-in the arts and sciences.

The literary writer Goethe did not stop at the door to the plant sciences, but instead continued to open doors of numerous other scientific disciplines, such as physics, meteorology, medicine and geology. For instance, the incisive bone, located just b ind our top incisors, is also known as 'Goethe's bone', as he was the first to prove its existence in mammals.

At the time of his death, Goethe had collected around 18,000 samples of rock in order to gain a complete understanding of the discipline of geology.

Interestingly, Goethe, who worked in both arts and sciences, was well aware of the gulf that had been widening between the two disciplines. Goethe considered that separating the two would make science more 'mechanistic and materialistic'.[26] He considered that science would be able to make greater progress if scientists continued to see the beauty of nature, and criticised the rise of scientists who were reluctant to leave their laboratories and failed to interact with the natural world.

If we were to summarise Goethe's approach towards learning, we could say with some certainty that knowledge, for Goethe, was not to be sliced, like a mango, but consumed like a grape—whole.

Meanwhile, back in Oxford at the student's gathering, Latika had left the party and Chetanya, relishing his slice of Alphonso mango, continued his lecture about the legendary Nikola Tesla (1856–1943) to the group.

I wish Chetanya had known that the prolific inventor Nikola Tesla—who is best known for designing the alternating-current-based (AC) electricity system and for his ambitious idea of wireless electricity—was also one of artist Goethe's greatest admirers, and had memorised *Faust* by heart. *Faust*, a tragic drama composed by Goethe, is considered to be one of the greatest works of German literature.[27]

In ancient Indian drama, a narrator (or *sutradhaar* in Hindi) usually appears at the beginning of the play, prays to the gods, and narrates the context of the play to the audience. Taking inspiration from the *Abhigyan Shakuntalam*, Goethe uses this technique at the beginning of *Faust*.

In *Faust*, a demon makes a bet with God that he can tempt God's favourite human (named Faust), and make him veer from the path of virtue. In Faust's case, the 'good life' meant learning all that is possible to learn. The demon manages to convince Faust to sell his soul to the devil in exchange for absolute knowledge.

It is said that Nikola Tesla—as he took one of his regular evening walks through the city parks of Budapest, the capital of Hungary—had an epiphany of sorts while reciting Goethe's *Faust*. It was precisely while his heart was immersed in the poetic narration of Goethe that his mind thought of the idea of an induction motor producing alternating current.[28]

Scientists Doing Arts
A Nobel laureate's conversation with the ancient musical instrument, mridanga

Nikola Tesla might have had an epiphany while reciting Goethe's *Faust*, yet a question remains, one that may be asked by hair-splitters like our dear friend Chetanya…

Does the epiphany episode really tell us about how exactly the arts inspire or contribute to science?

Chetanya's question compels us to travel many centuries back, to trace the astounding science b ind a humble musical instrument from ancient India—the mridanga. Once we have figuratively travelled through the great storms of war and historical enterprise, we will find that we are not the first to research the melodious nature of the mridanga. Chandras hara Venkata Raman, the first Indian to win a Nobel Prize in Physics, was there before us—perhaps to the surprise of many science students of current times, who may not be able to visualise scientists of significant stature spending time in the company of a musical instrument.

CV Raman, as the Nobel laureate is popularly addressed, is not the only one in his family to win the Nobel in Physics. His nephew, Subramanyan Chandras har, also won the coveted prize for his contribution to the study of the birth and death of a star. The twinkling stars that we see in the sky, including our Sun, seem to have existed for an eternity. However, the progress in stellar science—the field of study that deals with the death and birth of celestial bodies—teaches us that all our stars have a specific period of birth. And, as anything that is born also has to die, a star is not immortal. Subramanyan Chandras har contributed to our understanding of exactly when the process of a star's destruction commences.

Chandrash ar's uncle, CV Raman, was born in Tiruchirappalli (Trichy), a small town in southern India, in 1888, almost 430 years after the birth of Leonardo da Vinci and 140 years after Goethe. Although Raman won the Nobel Prize for identifying changes in the properties of light when it passes through a transparent medium (now known as the 'Raman effect'), in this chapter we will focus instead on his research into the science b ind the mridanga, a two-sided drum.

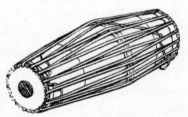

The ancient, two-sided Indian musical instrument, mridanga

CV Raman first presented his work on the mridanga to the world in 1920, in a brief two-page article that he published in the prestigious scientific journal *Nature*.[1] Fifteen years later, in 1935, Raman published an extensive analysis of the mridanga[2] in the *Proceedings of the Indian Academy of Sciences*.[3]

Upon reading both articles, I realised that in order to fully appreciate Raman's research on the mridanga, I would need to demolish all my watertight boundaries between 'arts' and 'sciences'. Because that is exactly what Raman had done: his research not only demonstrated his command of acoustics[4] and the development and manufacturing principles of musical instruments, but also the finer elements of musical composition (such as the *sur*, *taal*, *raga* and *shruti*), which only dedicated musicians can lay claim to understanding.

The moment I read the first paragraph of his article in *Nature*, my lack of knowledge of the interdisciplinary concepts, which the Nobel laureate freely delved in, was exposed:

> It is well known that percussion instruments as a class give inharmonic overtones, and are thus musically defective. We find on investigation that a special type of musical drum [mridanga] (emphasis added) which has long been known and used in India forms a very remarkable exception to the foregoing rule, as it gives harmonic overtones having the same relation of pitch to the fundamental tone as in stringed instruments.[5]

Like a perfect bouncer in a game of cricket, this paragraph went over my head! I had to spend a full day to make any sense of it. Like a primary school student, I felt that I had to start right from the very basics.

To understand how musical instruments can produce sound, and what Raman wrote, I decided to undertake a simple science project—the construction of a flute.

Flute is considered to be one of the oldest and simplest musical instruments known to human civilisation. A five-hole flute made from the wing bone of a vulture, discovered in Germany in 2008, is thought to be almost 35,000 years old.[6] In the ancient Indian epic text, Mahabharata, the flute is described as the favourite musical instrument of Lord Krishna.

In order to create a flute, we need a hollow, thinly walled piece from one of the stems of a bamboo tree.

To understand how a good flute works, let's first create a bad flute.

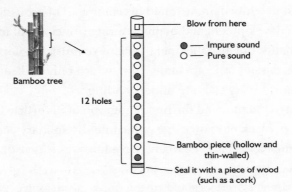

From a bamboo piece to a rudimentary flute

As shown in the above diagram, cut twelve circular holes on the hollow piece of bamboo, along with a rectangular hole near the top end. Seal the other end with a cork.

That's it.

Our bad flute is ready.

It is bad because out of the twelve holes, only six will produce a pure sound (tone), whereas the other six holes will produce impure versions of these tones.

For example, in classical Indian music, there are seven pure base tones (frequency of sound)—*sa, re, ga, ma, pa dha, ne*—the *sur,*[7] as it is termed in Sanskrit.

These seven tones are called 'harmonic fundamental frequencies' (or fundamental tones, as Raman addresses them in his article).

And in order to produce these seven *sur*s (tones), not twelve but only six holes in a flute are needed. For example, as shown in the next diagram, the seven *sur*s are produced by using various finger combinations over the six pure holes (for instance, the *sur* '*sa*' is produced when the top three holes are kept shut and the lower three holes are kept open).

I term these six holes pure because their creation is not random, but follows specific principles of the science of acoustics.

Thus, in order to create a good flute, a bamboo piece with specific length and width is to be chosen and, based on these parameters, six circular holes (tone holes) are to be cut at specific distances (corresponding to the length of the flute).[8]

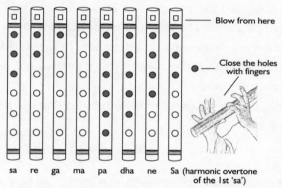

The finger movement to play harmonious tones (sur)

The above diagram also shows that after the seven *sur*s, the first *sur*, '*sa*', repeats itself. Sound travels in the form of waves and each *sur* has a fixed wavelength, and once the cycle is complete, the pattern repeats. Thus, after '*ne*', the next pure tone will again be '*Sa*', but with double the frequency of the fundamental '*sa*'. Thus, all pure tones other than the fundamental frequency (such as this second '*Sa*') are termed *overtones*. As these are pure overtones, these are also called harmonic overtones. Now, let's go back to our twelve-hole bad flute. Any sound that is produced between the six holes of pure tones (such as between '*sa*' and '*re*' or '*pa*' and '*dha*'), is considered an impure form (sharp or flat) or inharmonic tone.

In his article, Raman is talking about harmonic and inharmonic *sur*s in the context of percussion instruments.

Percussion instruments are those where we make sounds by thumping, tapping or striking their surface. Drums, the tabla and the mridanga are all examples of percussion instruments (whereas veena, sitar or guitar are examples of stringed instruments). Our vocal chords are a kind of a percussion instrument, with which we produce a sound by thumping our tongue (beatboxing is one such example).

If we now read the introductory paragraph of CV Raman's article again, we would be able to understand that the mridanga is the only percussion instrument in the world that is manufactured with such scientific precision that it does not produce inharmonic overtones.

It is this unique property of the mridanga that our beloved Nobel laureate delves into.

***

The earliest mridangas (or tannumais in Tamil) can be traced back to at least 3,500 years ago. Raman (1935) notes that cave paintings of mridangas have been found in the ancient Ajanta Caves in Maharashtra, India, and expresses his amazement at those who first created the instrument, calling it 'a remarkable testimony to the inventiveness and musical taste of its progenitors'.[9]

Students in India learn about the Ajanta Caves in school, but I do feel that we are made aware of these without making us realise that these caves are the equivalent of the pyramids of Egypt and the ruins of Rome, to which millions of tourists flock each year.

In order to appreciate the astounding nature of the Ajanta Caves, imagine that you have been given a small piece of rock and are asked to sculpt it into a miniature house with rooms.

I am certain the task would take many months to complete, not to mention the tools and skill set of a sculptor! The Ajanta Caves came into being around 200 BC,[10] when a solid, 76-metre high (equivalent to a 25-storey building) and 250-metre long rock, deep in the jungles of Maharashtra, was sculpted to create 30 magnificent caves. Hollowed out from the inside over centuries, the rock was finally transformed into a piece of art dedicated to the teachings of Buddha. A symbol of architectural brilliance, the Ajanta Caves consist of several chambers, each of which comprises spectacular pillars, domes, intricate floral patterns and statues, all carved from the rock.

The cave walls are ornamented with magnificent paintings. And on one such walls, CV Raman had spotted a mridanga.

The word mridanga is actually a compound word, combining *mrida* (meaning clay) and *angam* (meaning body part). This is because the earliest version of the mridanga was created by heating clay to a very high temperature, much like an earthen pot.

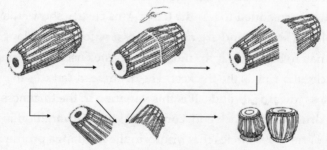

Transformation of mridanga into the tabla

Being illiterate in music, I had never noticed that the mridanga is not symmetrical in form: if we were to split the instrument in two, the right side would be different from the left, both in terms of structure and the sound it makes. According to Raman, this asymmetry inspired musicians in later centuries to invent another instrument, the tabla, which is essentially a mridanga that has been divided in two and placed on the floor to be played as two separate instruments.

The Nobel laureate, amazed by the scientific brilliance of the creators of this ancient instrument, goes into great detail to explain the structural engineering of the mridanga and the process of creating its right-side drumhead,[11] which only produces harmonic overtones.

As Raman elaborates, the circular, right-hand drumhead is 'not a single piece of leather, but consists of three layers of drum-skin superposed on each other'. In the final stages of the instrument's construction, the right-hand side is made up of three skins that are separated by metal rings. The width of these rings is adjusted to suit the instrument's harmonic requirements. A paste made up of iron oxide, charcoal, starch and gum is then applied to the top layer of the three-layered drumhead. The application of the paste is not a simple process and requires careful precision—it is applied layer by layer, and the drumhead is played after each layer has been added to test the tones. This clearly shows the interplay of science and art, as it is necessary for the mridanga craftsman to have an ear for music. The paste ensures the central, dark, circular ring is the thickest. The drumhead reduces in thickness towards its ends. It is this variation in the thickness of the drumhead at each end, combined with the variation in width of the three circles that results in the mridanga producing harmonic overtones when tapped and thumped with various combinations of the fingers and palm.

As I read the intricate explanation of the eminent scientist, an image of a time-travelled CV Raman, standing in front of a mridanga maker sitting in a 3500-year-old ancient Indian village marketplace, diligently observing the mridanga being built, was superimposed in my mind.

But as my eyes turn to the floor, I realised that the mridanga is not much of an attention se er; perhaps that is the reason why so many in contemporary India do not know about it.

But then, like a selfless river that flows every day and helps those living close to it to flourish without any expectations of its own, the mridanga too has always done its job without needing to boast about its remarkable capabilities.

As our time travelling comes to an end, the ancient, humble mridanga lays itself bare, in the hope that after hearing its story we may dismantle those boxes caging arts and sciences and allow them to flow together.

Businessmen Doing
Arts And Sciences

How iPhone's journey starts in the year 1837 and passes through the ashrams of India

Just as the artist Rishi continued with only his imagined right-brain thinking, and Chetanya, the scientist enclosed his thoughts in another box where no artist was welcome, Rahul and his father made sure to keep everyone and everything that didn't translate into business out of their respective worlds—yet, in spite of breathing business day in and day out, Rahul's start-up venture failed.

Rahul, with his chained understanding of business, may not have been ready to listen to reasons why Pigeon stopped flying from an artist or a scientist but, perhaps, there is one person whom he cannot choose to ignore. In fact, his father, too, would be quite keen to get into his mind—after all he was one of the richest people in the world, and that, too, without any formal education.

But this person, unlike Chetanya, would very likely have loved to carry on the discussion with the Bharatanatyam dancer, Latika. Even Jaighosh would have given his tooth and nail to have a conversation with him as he is the *one* who conceptualised the place where Jaighosh dreams of working.

He is the legendary Steve Jobs.

The businessman Steve Jobs co-founded Apple Inc. when he was only twenty-one. We are right to call him a businessman, as he created what is now one of the most valued companies in the world!

If Apple were a person, at its current age of forty-one, it would be much younger than Rahul's father. We know Rahul's father's views on how business is carried out and how a businessman should think, but Apple's achievement tempts me to wonder how Steve Jobs thought and what he did to create one of the biggest corporations in the world.

Let's run some numbers to measure the business acumen of Steve Jobs before we take any lessons from him. As the next table shows, Apple is currently valued at US$ 910 billion (approximately 60 lac crore).[1] Just to grasp this enormous number, when compared to the US$ 186.59-billion-worth (approximately 12.3 lac crore),[2] 126-year-old Coca Cola company—it would take approximately five Coca Cola companies to match Apple's worth!

Relative to businesses in India, Apple's value is approximately equivalent to nine times that of Tata Consultancy Services (TCS), which recently became the first Indian company to touch US$ 100-billion market valuation (approximately 6.6 lac crore),[3] the most valued Indian company, and twenty-four times (US$ 38-billion-worth or approximately 2.5 lac crore) that of the State Bank of India (SBI),[4] the largest public-sector bank in India.

Rahul's father, with his sand mine and wheat export business, seems quite a rich person. If we were to assume his net worth at even, let's say, 200 crore (approximately US$ 31 million), we would need to assemble at least 29,000 rich businessmen like him to match Apple's value!

Name of Company	Market Value (in US$)	Age in 2018	Comparison to Apple Inc.
Apple Inc.	US$ 910 billion	42 years	
Coca Cola	US$ 186.59 billion	125 years	1 Apple = 5 Coca Cola
TCS (Tata Consultancy Services)	US$ 92 billion	49 years	1 Apple = 10 TCS
SBI (State Bank of India	US$ 38 billion	211 years	1 Apple = 24 SBI
Rahul's father's net worth	US$ 31 million	55 years	1 Apple = 29,000 Rahul's father's net worth

Apple's net worth comparisons

These numbers are a dazzling reflection of Jobs' stature as a remarkable businessman. But the journey of one of the most successful businessmen in the world shows that he did not achieve this by restricting himself only to the subject island of business. In fact, it was Steve Jobs' willingness to move beyond the boundaries of science, art and business that resulted in the creation of the most valuable business enterprise in the world.

***

On 9 January 2007, when Steve Jobs presented the first version of the iPhone to the world, it became a revolutionary moment in the history of communication.[5] In the past ten years, smartphones have become the largest-selling electronic item on planet Earth, and the iPhone has even been considered the number-one gadget ever built by human civilisation.[6] It is this particular product that has helped Apple become the most valuable company in the world.

Incidentally, Rahul started Pigeon with the desire to create a successful start-up that could produce iPhone lookalikes. But then, Rahul's Pigeon is not alone; once iPhone came into the market with its unique flat-screen, front-face, all-glass interface design in 2007, cheap copies of it have been mushrooming all around the world.[7]

Since its first model, Apple has been regularly upgrading the iPhone.[8] While Steve Jobs was alive, he personally headed the iPhone design team. But this raises an important question: can an 'uneducated' person design-lead one of the most popular smartphones of our time, which is not only aesthetically pleasing but also capable of accommodating continuously progressing smartphone technology—and if so, can he be called uneducated?

This question compels us to look at the fixed mindset we have regarding the definition of education: anyone who goes through the formal process of school and college is considered to be educated and those without a degree, the opposite.

But then, sometimes, the formal process doesn't result in much learning, but many a time the learning of a degreeless person is exemplary. These qualification-less people, like Jobs, are indeed passionate about learning but often refuse to acquire a degree or the label of a specialist.

And, perhaps as a blessing in disguise, with no pressure of the requirement of a formal qualification to walk on a fixed path, they manage to learn freely, going beyond labels and disciplinary boundaries, and often end up acquiring valuable, diverse knowledge.

This is exactly what happened in the case of Steve Jobs.

In order to understand the true depth of Jobs' knowledge,

I decided to explore how Jobs managed to create the iPhone without acquiring a formal degree.

This process took me to the door of a simple question—not a complicated theory or principle from science, arts or business, but a much simpler question: why a KG standard is called KG, or kindergarten?

We can be pretty certain that anybody reading this book would have passed the KG exam (or its equivalent), but how many would know or even want to know why kindergarten is called kindergarten?

In fact, our education has reached to a state where most of us keep collecting qualifications or degree labels without questioning what we learn and why we learn as we go along.

Not many so-called educated people among us would know the answer to the KG question; but, perhaps, the uneducated Steve Jobs does, because in the answer to this question is hidden the path of iPhone creation.

The answer takes us to the year 1837. This may seem far, far back in history, but for me this was the year when the foundation for the iPhone was actually laid.

***

It was in 1837 that Friedrich Fröbel, a German scholar working in the field of education, not only coined the term kindergarten[9] but also established the first kindergarten.

Kindergarten (or KG) is a German compound word, combining *kinder* (children)[10] and *garten* (garden).

Around the beginning of the nineteenth century, the modern education system started to bring the pressure of learning into classrooms—but no one knew where to draw the line; that is, at what age a child can start dealing with this type of pressure.

Fröbel believed that children should not be forced to learn

but instead be allowed to explore the world on their own. To put it simply, a kindergarten should be a garden for children—just as a flower grows in a garden, a child should be able to grow in a kindergarten.

In Fröbel's kindergarten, a child would do gardening, take care of pets, and learn through playing games.

In fact, it was Fröbel who popularised the concept of singing nursery rhymes to children! However, the rhymes were not meant to be parroted back by the children, as we so often see today, but rather make them feel happy and fall in love with learning.

For Fröbel, every mother must be trained to understand the importance of unforced learning, and every home should be a lovable garden for children, devoid of punishment—a kindergarten.

According to Fröbel, learning was not only to be achieved by reading books—playing with a simple toy could be the most important educational activity for young children.

For example, Fröbel proposed that a ball should be introduced to a child as soon as he or she is three months old. This ball would familiarise the infant with the concepts of space, time and movement, stimulating its imagination from a young age.

Incidentally, Fröbel, the educator, was not told that his job was to remain in the shell of a teacher; he was fluid and hence he crossed over to manufacture a set of toys comprising balls, cubes, spheres, cylinders and geometric building blocks. These are now known as Fröbel gifts.

Thus, in Fröbel's kindergarten, learning materials were toys that brought joy to children. In Fröbel's world, a child should not be punished into going to school but should be pulled towards it by attractive and fun learning.

Incidentally, Fröbel gifts, the creations of an educationist, inspired Danish carpenter Ole Kirk Christiansen (1891–1958) to create LEGO®, the multibillion-dollar building block toy brand, with which many children of today play.

Fröbel's kindergarten started a movement of sorts in the USA, where hundreds of kindergartens opened in the second half of the nineteenth century.

In 1876, a primary school teacher named Anna Lloyd Jones attended an exhibition on education in Philadelphia, USA, where Fröbel gifts were being displayed. Anna Lloyd Jones bought a set of these gifts from the exhibition for her son, Frank Lloyd Wright, who went on to become one of the most influential architects in the world.

Frank Lloyd Wright (1867–1959) states the influence that Fröbel gifts had on him in his autobiography:

> [...] for several years I sat at the little kindergarten table-top ruled by lines about four inches apart each way making four-inch squares; and among other things, played upon these 'unit lines' with the square (cube), the circle (sphere) and the triangle (tetrahedron or tripod) [...] Eventually I was to construct designs in other mediums. But the smooth cardboard triangles and maple wood blocks were most important. *All are in my fingers to this day* [emphasis added].[11]

Inspired by the influence that Fröbel gifts had exerted on his young mind, Wright brought linearity and geometrical simplicity to building design. Where fashionable building façades had previously been heavily decorated, with steep sloping roofs and protruding bay windows, in Wright's designs they were simple geometric shapes.

Wright also coined the term 'organic architecture', which referred to a house or a building that, when constructed, becomes a part of the landscape and not an exception to it, thus upholding the principles of environmental protection. One house designed by Wright, named *Fallingwater*, achieved iconic status[12] (considered to be the 'best all-time work of American architecture'), as it sat on top of a natural waterfall and was enveloped all around by greenery, so that it appeared as if it had been erected by nature itself.

Incidentally, Ayn Rand took inspiration from Frank Lloyd Wright and sketched the character of Howard Roark—the protagonist/architect in *The Fountainhead*—on how Wright was in his real life. One of the buildings by Roark in the masterpiece novel is based on Wright's *Fallingwater*.

A house with heavily decorated façade
↓

Fallingwater: An iconic house designed by Frank Wright with linear façade and utilising principles of 'organic architecture'
↓

One of the buildings by Eichler, a Californian real-estate developer, inspired by Wright's design principles with simple rectangular façade and floor-to-ceiling glass walls.

The geometric linearity introduced by Frank Lloyd Wright resulted in buildings with floor-to-ceiling glass façades. Steve Jobs spent his childhood in one such house and drew inspiration to bring this style to Apple products.

As shown in the previous illustration, Fröbel's simple gifts didn't only influence Wright. Joseph Eichler (1900–1974), a prominent real estate developer in California, USA, who built more than 11,000 houses in his lifetime, brought Wright's linear design philosophy to mass housing.[13]

Eichler's homes were typically open plan and linear in form, and comprised exposed beams and glass walls.

It was in one such home that Steve Jobs spent his childhood. Jobs' childhood home made him fall in love with the power of Eichler's simple and clean designs. He communicated to his biographer, Walter Isaacson (2011:7), the scale of Eichler's impact on the design principles of Apple products:

> Eichler did a great thing [...] his houses [...] brought clean design and simple taste to lower-income people [...] It was the original vision for Apple. That's what we tried to do with the first Mac. That's what we did with the iPod.[14]

Having stumbled upon this connection between Friedrich Fröbel, Frank Lloyd Wright, Joseph Eichler and Steve Jobs, I glanced at my iPhone and it appeared itself to be a miniature, rectangular, white building designed following the principles of geometric linearity. And its front screen appeared exactly like Eichler's floor-to-ceiling glass façades!

Perhaps this chain of connections, which started from 1837, also inspired Jobs to conceptualise the circular Apple Park with all-curved glass elevation.

As shown in the next illustration, if I now look at Apple Park, it appears to be a giant, Fröbelian kindergarten ball with a mini-forest at its centre, following Wright's principles of organic architecture and enveloped inside Eichler's floor-to-ceiling glass walls.

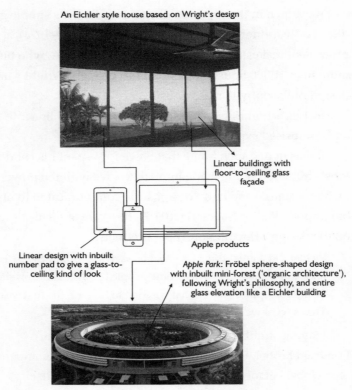

An Eichler style house based on Wright's design

Linear buildings with floor-to-ceiling glass façade

Apple products

Linear design with inbuilt number pad to give a glass-to-ceiling kind of look

Apple Park: Fröbel sphere-shaped design with inbuilt mini-forest ('organic architecture'), following Wright's philosophy, and entire glass elevation like a Eichler building

The transformation of Fröbel Gifts, Wright's architectural principles and Eichler's buildings into Apple products

How Fröbel's simple geometric toys inspired the linear design principles of Frank Wright, which were reflected in one of the Eichler homes in which Steve Jobs spent his childhood, before carrying that linearity on into Apple products.

***

The 'uneducated' Steve Jobs not only drew inspiration from several fields, but also broke a couple of those narrow approaches we adopt as a result of our formal process of education.

Think about the time when we choose our subjects after our tenth standard at school. This decision also steers our friendships. Our classroom arrangements separate us from those who have chosen to take other disciplines. We start to spend more time with those who study with us. This gap between those not taking the same subjects and us widens even further when we enter college.

How often does a medical student spend time with a commerce or an engineering student?

For reunions and alumni meetings, the trend continues to divide us by discipline even after college. And now, thanks to Whatsapp groups, we find ourselves again speaking with the same set of people. Offline or online, we spend our time with similar kinds of people, who all do similar things, have an interest in similar topics and even, more often than not, fall in love from within our circle of acquaintances.

It is quite often when we see a doctor insisting on marrying another doctor, or, as we saw in the case of Rahul, an MBA wanting to spend his social time in the company of those who want to discuss money!

We assume that spending time in our network opens up opportunities for us.

But fluid Steve Jobs breaks this myth.

At the age of six, Jobs moved with his adoptive parents to a neighbourhood in Mountain View, California, in the heart of Silicon Valley. It was full of engineers and the children of the area were naturally exposed to engineering subjects. Thus, the first set of friends that Jobs had were children of engineers.

A few years later, the family bought a house in a nearby neighbourhood that had even more engineers than the previous one did, and amidst this circle of friends Jobs leaned towards an education in technology.

Some may assume that being surrounded by engineering friends was the biggest reason b ind Jobs' success, and they may even be tempted to move to an area similarly populated with engineers. But such people should think before they start packing, as that is not what Steve Jobs did.

People often say that Jobs was a college dropout, but it is rarely mentioned that his college contributed significantly in helping him to see a world beyond engineering.

Jobs had enrolled at Reed College, Oregon, almost 1,000 km north of Silicon Valley. Reed is a liberal arts college and, although Jobs dropped out after the first year of study, it was enough for him to get a taste of the world beyond science and technology. In his words:

> I discovered Shakespeare, Dylan Thomas, and all that classic stuff. I read Moby Dick and went back as a junior taking creative writing classes…I started to listen to music a whole lot, and I started to read more outside of just science and technology—Shakespeare, Plato.[15]

After entering the liberal arts college, Jobs maintained two circles of friends—those who talked about changing the world through science and technology, and those who discussed the profoundness of art and literature. In fact, Jobs was described by someone who knew him from his student years as:

> …kind of a brain and kind of a hippie…but he never fit into either group.[16]

Jobs' approach was precisely opposite to that of Chetanya, who never considered extending his friendship circle beyond scientists and technocrats. And this fluid attitude towards friendship also helped Jobs in arriving at the cutting-edge design of Apple products.

At Reed, Steve Jobs met Daniel Kottke, with whom he came on a spiritual journey to India and stayed there for seven months. The influence of this journey was so deep that, when he returned to the USA, he had shaved his head and begun to wear traditional Indian clothing.[17] In India, Jobs developed a genuine affection for South Indian music. It is said that he listened to South Indian music on a loop while creating the first-ever Mac computer.[18]

This is precisely the reason why, unlike Chetanya, Jobs would have loved to interact with Latika, and might have asked her a thing or two about Bharatanatyam.

Importantly, Jobs' stay in the ashrams of India taught him the importance of simplicity. Jobs even travelled to Japan, where he developed a deep appreciation for Buddhism. His open approach and willingness to expose himself to various cultures helped him bring new perspectives to the world of design and engineering. His visits to India and Japan reinforced the importance of clear, minimalistic and simple designs, which he had picked up from his childhood residence.

Jobs' inclination towards the colour white was also driven by the principle of simplicity. When Apple started its journey, most technology companies made their products in black. Black was used to dazzle customers, to tell them they were buying something complex and highly technical. Steve Jobs took the inspiration for designing his products in white from Braun—the electronics and home appliances company. He said:

> We will make them bright and pure and honest about being high-tech, rather than a heavy industrial look of black, black, black, black, like Sony.[19]

Jobs not only interacted with people from the other camp, but his exposure to arts shaped his design philosophies. In his famous speech (known as 'connecting the dots') to a group of Stanford University graduates in the year 2005, Jobs mentioned the influence that taking a calligraphy class at Reed College had on his career:

> If I had never dropped in on that single calligraphy course in college, the Mac would have never had multiple typefaces or proportionally

spaced fonts...[At Reeds] I learned about serif and sans serif typefaces, about varying the amount of space between different letter combinations, about what makes great typography great. It was beautiful, historical, artistically subtle in a way that science can't capture, and I found it fascinating.[20]

Looking at the diverse knowledge that Jobs gathered and translated into his products, it would be unjustified to call him uneducated.

But then Steve Jobs, who achieved a remarkable feat in translating building designs into computer and mobile devices, is often touted as a hero by those who assume that education is a waste of time. It is not that Rahul's father or thousands of similar businessmen do not believe in what they say—the problem is that they truly think that the college dropout Steve Jobs created Apple with no education.

Perhaps this is precisely what happens when we don't go deeper into a subject but only read the news headlines. But this is, to use Neil deGrasse Tyson's words again, simply lazy.

Yes, Steve Jobs dropped out of college, but this was largely an outcome of uninspiring classrooms. And Jobs compensated for this lack of classroom learning by treating the world as a classroom, where imagination, experience and self-inquiry drove his learning.

For example, Steve Jobs' self-made syllabus exposed him to the life of another college dropout, Edwin Land, who was so scientifically advanced that at the time of his death he held 535 patents,[21] the world's second-highest number of patents held by anyone.[22]

Edwin Land (1909–1991) is popularly known as the founder of the Polaroid Corporation. Polaroid revolutionised photography by releasing a camera that could produce photographic prints on demand. Before Polaroid, a typical camera had a photo reel, which had to be taken to a photo-development laboratory (commonly known in India as a 'colour lab') for the photographs to be printed. Polaroid technology became such a hit that, in the year 1978 alone, 14.3 million (1.43 crore) Polaroid cameras were sold![23]

In India, Polaroid enticed thousands of small-time photographers, who previously could not afford expensive colour labs but now had a device that could give them a decent livelihood.

Photographers on bicycles with cameras hanging from their necks were then frequently spotted riding on dusty trails that led to the remotest of villages, places that had no electricity, required for making passport-size photographs.

Land had dropped out of Harvard, but filed his first patent at the age of nineteen, and went on to establish a company that would sell the highest number of instant camera units in the world.

When Land became Steve Jobs' hero, Jobs must have had two choices: either he could stop himself at the headlines and carry on with the knowledge that a college dropout had managed to create a billion-dollar company, or he could dig deeper and find out how Land did it. Unlike Rahul's father, Steve Jobs did not stop at the headlines—he spent considerable time learning the reasons for Land's success and embraced this crossover definition of business. Jobs found the college dropout Land to be more educated than many graduates he knew. In Jobs' words:

> [Meeting Land was]…like visiting a shrine…[Edwin Land] saw the intersection of art and science and business and built an organisation to reflect that.[24]

Both Steve Jobs and Edwin Land teach us to remain fluid, to not to fall for the stereotypical definition of a businessman. Sadly, the current boxed approach of formal education has taken those pursuing commerce far from interacting with other disciplines. Perhaps this is the reason Rahul simply refused to believe that Priya could also bring valuable business insight to the table, and why Priya did not let Rahul enter her world of technology. And then there was Fatima, whose interest in science fiction went misunderstood by both Rahul and Priya.

Today, start-ups are considered to be the largest source of the next generation of jobs, and an MBA the most sought-after degree. But a question arises: does education for business only happen b ind the closed doors of business schools, through a curriculum obsessed only with the teaching of business?

At least it doesn't look like that when we ponder the success of Steve Jobs. The college-dropout founder of the most valuable company in the world serves us up his self-cooked B-school curriculum. It begins by telling us to always learn without any pressure of failure, almost how a three-month-old child would learn with a simple Fröbelian toy. It requests us to take inspiration from our surroundings as he did from his childhood home and teaches us to embrace friends from the worlds of all disciplines. B-school curriculum of Steve Jobs doesn't stop us from searching for spirituality in the ashrams of India or backpacking and exploring the world or living like a hermit near the gardens in Kyoto, Japan—it encourages us to appreciate diverse cultures and philosophies, and even learn calligraphy or spend hours listening to classical music.

Above all, to be able to learn business, the counter-intuitive fluid B-school curriculum of Steve Jobs urges us to step out of the very box of business, inside which, the real B-schools are unknowingly trying to paste us.

The Dangers Of Entering Machine Age With An Anti-fluid Mind

Our Lives And Careers
From Hereon

It can be all be fascinating to read about da Vinci, Goethe, Raman, Jobs or Land—the fluid ones—but why should it change the way we currently live our lives or devise our careers or become specialists?

The gat eepers of our careers can very well argue that the reason specialists become specialists is precisely because they remain focused, because they take the decision to not be disturbed by any unrelated knowledge. Why should someone such as a cardiologist or a cancer specialist or a scientist or an IT specialist or an architect or a lawyer or an economist be bothered to cross over the boundaries of their subject when they are already achieving success without needing to do so?

And hence we copy. We copy those who have followed the formula. We set paths of our education, set trajectories of our careers—after all, we all know what works and what doesn't: the top ranked universities, the most sought-after fields. We have worked it all out to the last dot.

It could have all remained perfectly fine but for the arrival of the ones who can copy better.

Welcome to the age of machines.

The Ones Who Can Copy Better

Dr Watson from New York, USA is quite famous. Dr Watson trained to be a lung, breast and colorectal cancer diagnostic expert and is known for accuracy in the line of treatment a cancer patient requires. Recently, in order to test Dr Watson's reputation, the Manipal Comprehensive Cancer Center, situated in Bengaluru, India, conducted a large-scale study of 638 patients of Dr Watson, and were amazed to find that while a usual cancer specialist would take twenty minutes to arrive at a diagnosis, it took only forty seconds for Dr Watson to identify the type and stage of cancer and recommend a line of treatment.[1]

The only small detail here is that Dr Watson is not a human but a machine.

Watson is IBM's advanced computer, which was trained by the oncologists at the Memorial Sloan Kettering Cancer Center, New York, USA, for the past five years to become an intelligent cancer diagnostic expert. In cancer treatment, personalised, evidence-based treatment is crucial, which in simple terms means that each patient needs to be treated on the basis of his personal, specific health condition. Over the past several years, like a sincere medical student, Watson mastered the compr ensive curriculum. In no time, it had already memorised over 1.5 million patient records and data from clinical trials, as well as reading over two million pages of advanced medical journals. Based on its learning and using its sophisticated analytical brain, Dr Watson is able to compare patients' genetics, family history and treatments given, and is able to suggest a specific line of treatment with remarkable accuracy.

Then there is one Mr Ross in the field of law. A 2017 *New York Times* article[2] cites the example of Luis Salazar, a lawyer-partner in a small law firm, who after hearing about Mr Ross decided to test its abilities. Salazar was working on a particular case and wanted to find out whether a similar case had reached the courts before. First, he decided to work without the assistance of Mr Ross. It took Salazar ten hours of internet research, but he managed to locate a very similar case. Then he outsourced the same problem to Mr Ross. According to Salazar, Mr Ross pointed to the similar case in no time.

Both Dr Watson and Mr Ross tell us how copying may not work anymore as we enter the machine age.

***

If the prediction of Deloitte's research wing (one of the largest consulting companies in the world) comes true, the likes of Mr Ross may cost humans more than 100,000 jobs in the legal field within the next ten years in the USA alone.

Before the beginning of the twenty-first century, the far-fetched, dangerous prediction that the time is not far off when most of the jobs will be snatched away from humans by intelligent machines remained largely confined to the scientific community or perhaps the die-hard fans of science fiction, like our dear Fatima—the first employee of Pigeon.

As the first decade of the twenty-first century came to an end, a larger section of the population started waking up to the threatening reality and the all-important buzzword—artificial intelligence.

In 2013, an Oxford University study[3] started getting widely cited by news media around the world, setting alarm bells ringing among those at the early stages of their career. The study examined 702 job categories in the USA and concluded that, in the next twenty years, 47 per cent of jobs are at risk of being taken away from humans due to automation.

The dangers of machine replacement are not illusory if we look at the efforts of people like Art Bilger, a board member at Wharton business school and a venture capitalist based in the USA, who has founded an NGO called Working Nation, precisely for educating the American public to prepare them against the risk of redundancy brought in by the robots.

Most developed nations have woken up to the threat of machine invasion. For example, in Japan, The Nomura Research Institute has predicted that robots could replace nearly half of the country's jobs by the year 2035.[4]

The National Bureau of Economic Research (NBER), USA, claims that the threat of machines is not only real but has already begun. NBER examined the job scenario in the US manufacturing sector between 1990 and 2007, only to realise that each robot hired replaced 6.2 humans.

The impact of the machines can be seen in almost all sectors, which we can understand through a few examples mentioned below.

If we start with the insurance sector, Fukoku Mutual Life Insurance, a Japanese insurance company, recently announced that it has already laid off some of its employees; their work is now to be done by an artificially intelligent machine. The work of these people was, essentially, to calculate payoffs for the firm's policyholders. As a result of replacing humans with a machine, the insurance company expected its productivity to be increased by 30 per cent.[5]

The food industry is not far b ind, as the first fully automated restaurant in the world has already opened its doors in San Francisco, USA. With no serving or administrative staff, *Eatsa*, the health-food restaurant, aims to spread all over the USA.[6]

The news of the impact of automation on the banking sector is now quite old. Tellers around the world have been tumbling like ninepins—that is, the cashiers handing out cash, which are always there whenever we think of a bank, are no longer required. Most of the work done by tellers is now automated. An article in the *Washington Post* (2017) announced the decision of the Bank of America to open robo-banks—branches with no humans. The article's headline ominously read, 'Bank tellers are the next blacksmiths.'[7]

As threatening as it may sound, automation will not stop at the teller level. The next in line are bank officers.

In fact, not only bank officers but administrative staff in most industries is at serious risk as well. The Oxford study asserted that by 2034 most mid-level jobs would see humans replaced by machines.

In the past few years, whenever I read those full-page newspaper ads for coaching centres, enticing the young population to get trained for the job of either a bank cashier or a bank officer, or a typical mediocre business school boasting its placement figures, I dearly wished to point all such prospective students towards literature on artificial intelligence and its impact on the future of jobs.

Currently, in India, a large section of the populace still

aspires to work in the government and semi-government sectors. This is largely due to the fact that they believe there is no apparent threat of lay-off. As little research has been done on how automation and digitalisation is reducing creation of new jobs in the government sector, such warnings are still not out. However, we only have to look at what is happening around the world to realise how soon the situation might change, even in such a secure sector. Take, for instance, the case of the person who comes to your house to take the water, gas and electricity readings. With the installation of smart metres and sensory chips on the pipelines, the day is not far off when no such person will be required to physically visit the houses. But then, this is only an example of someone with a small job and the officials at the top may never be convinced that machines can ever threaten their jobs.

Interestingly, many among us who work or aspire to work in high-demand sectors (such as medicine, engineering, investment banking, etc.) invariably think that our well-cushioned jobs are surely not in danger. We may be in for a rude shock, if we are to believe Moshe Vardi, a computer science professor at Rice University who forecast that by 2045, intelligent machines would be able to do each and every job that a human being is capable of.[8]

This clearly means that whether we are a specialist doctor or an expert engineer or a high-profile banker, none of us are safe.

For instance, in the field of medicine—probably the safest career option in India—one only has to look at advancements happening in robotic surgeries, diagnostics, patient monitoring and patient record management, etc. to understand the true impact of automation.

In fact, not only are there robotic lawyers like Mr Ross, but work is already in progress to develop a sophisticated machine judge that can deliver judgements with accuracy. Recently, scientists from the University of Pennsylvania, the University of Sheffield and University College, London, created one such machine. When given the task of predicting the outcomes already delivered in 584 cases previously heard at the European Court of Human Rights (ECHR), the machine judge displayed 79% accuracy.[9]

Similarly, a common phenomenon seen among those working in the field of arts is their lack of concern towards the risk of automation. This is largely due to the prevalence of this thought that machines will never attain the creative sophistication of a human being.

However, the reality is that in the past couple of decades, the impact of automation on the field of arts has been substantial.

Let's take a simple example of designing a website.

While previously a typical website-design project demanded months of creative input and multiple people, today a single good resource can build a decent website from scratch within a day.

Likewise, the intelligent machines have started showing potential for designing those products that were previously thought to be highly complex. For example, the first self-designed car exclusively by robots is already here.[10]

Further, the advent of 3D printers not only means that machines can design a product, but they can also manufacture it without the requirement of a full-fledged factory.

The risk of automation combined with 3D printing for many existing jobs is paramount.

Take, for instance, the case of the construction and housing industry, which employs a large section of the working population. As per the 2001 Census, India's working population was around 40 crore (400 million), out of which 16 per cent of people, i.e., roughly 6.4 crore (64 million), worked in the construction or related industries.[11] A typical housing project in India, let's say a six-story building with 100 apartments, takes roughly three to four years to complete. The project would typically require the services of more than 100 people, ranging from engineers, consultants, architects, project managers, surveyors, labourers, etc. Other than this, a section of government officers would be required to approve the project and monitor its progress. It is also often seen that, due to various external factors (severe weather conditions, poor management, high interest cost on loans, delay in government approvals, etc.), such a project gets delayed by several years, causing agony and financial loss to the intended buyers.

Now with the advent of automation and 3D printing, it is entirely possible to complete such a project with almost a tenth of the workforce. This may not be a fantasy if we know what happened in Dubai. In May 2017, in Dubai, a 20-feet-high, 120-feet-long, 40-feet-wide 3D printer with a giant robotic arm took on the task of creating a building entirely on its own.[12] After just seventeen days, Dubai became the first place in the world to see a fully functional office built entirely with a 3D printer.

Beyond the field of design, machines have also started penetrating into other creative fields. For example, a machine developed by Google has already composed its first song.

Similarly, creative writing, which was considered up to now out of the reach of machines, has received its first taste of competition. Recently, in Japan, an artificially intelligent robot was charged with writing a short novel. Not only was the novel written, but it was written well! Aptly titled *The Day a Computer Writes a Novel*, the written work cleared the first round of the Nikkei Hoshi Shinichi Literary Award, beating hundreds of entries submitted by humans.[13]

To sum up, with the arrival of driverless cars, self-writing computer programmes, 3D-printed products, automated surgeries, etc., it is not hard to see that the workplace of the future will change dramatically.

The technological progress of the next twenty years may render a large portion of the population jobless, or would certainly require them to at least plan their career in a completely different manner to the way they have been planning up to now.

So, how do we plan our lives against the ones who can copy better?

How about starting our quest with a story? The story of a girl named Yogini. It may sound bizarre that we are using storytelling to tackle the nuts and bolts and binary world of machines. After all, we have heard that it is the job of people from the world of technology and not storytellers to prepare us against machines.

So shouldn't we start our journey with a predetermined path?

But then, if we copy, if our journeys are predetermined and not fluid, how different are we from a machine itself?

Yogini, Shakespeare, Mimicking And Machines

Watching her father and the career counsellor embroiled in an argument over her future as if she were not even in the room almost made Yogini reach for the paperweight lying right in front of her. In spite of her stalwart father's presence, Yogini was quite capable of throwing the paperweight with full force and smashing whatever was smash-able in that room. Dr Roy, Yogini's father, had already had a taste of her medicine. That is why he even made an effort, although very reluctantly, to meet the supposed best career counsellor in Kolkata.

Dr Roy, one of the most famous cardiothoracic surgeons in the eastern region of India, was a fifth-generation doctor. In fact, most of the people in Yogini's family were doctors. Orthopaedic surgeons, paediatricians, neurologists, nephrologists, gynaecologists: you name the specialisation and it could be found in one of their extended family connections.

There was a three-month waiting period if one wanted to undergo heart surgery at Dr Roy's hands. And when one managed to get into Dr Roy's plush chamber, one couldn't ignore his great-great-grandfather's life-size portrait, in which he was holding an earlier version of the scalpel and was all ready to dissect a cadaver.

'Do you know who Madhusudan Gupta was?'

Whenever a young surgeon came to him to se his blessings and happened to stare at the magnificent portrait, Dr Roy made sure to ask his favourite rhetorical question.

'India wouldn't have seen any modern-day surgeons like us if Dr Madhusudan Gupta did not come forward and did what he did. He was the first Indian to dissect a human corpse.'

Although constantly hard-pressed for time, Dr Roy always found time to narrate the heroics of Madhusudan Gupta, 'It was 1835 when the first medical college was set up in India. However, the anatomy department of India's first medical college faced a peculiar problem—there was no one willing to dissect a dead human body. It was a major social taboo and months went by without any practical lessons, but Madhusudan, in spite of being a pundit, demonstrated courage and paved the way. It happened on 28 October 1836!'[1] He would continue pointing to the man holding the scalpel in the portrait, 'My great-great-grandfather was one of the classmates of Madhusudan Gupta. One among the first forty-nine medical students of India!'

Dr Roy's illustrious legacy was sufficient reason for him to think that Yogini, his only child, would not think of any career other than being a doctor.

However, Yogini was exactly the opposite of what Dr Roy imagined his child to be like.

Yogini loved to break every rule written in modern Indian society's book. Yogini was not even her real name, but one she had adopted on one of her journeys to Nepal. She was deeply immersed into yoga, Sufism, Buddhism and spirituality. Although she was only in class XII, Yogini had already backpacked alone to monasteries in Ladakh, Dharamshala and even to the one in Tengboche, a remote village situated in the foothills of the Himalaya in north-eastern Nepal. She had a new name when she left Tengboche.

It was not that Yogini did not like sciences—in fact, human evolution was her favourite subject—but the idea of being a doctor was what she hated most.

'It is almost like being on a factory conveyor belt.' It was a few months ago and Yogini had just returned from Tengboche when, for the first time, she revealed to Dr Roy her repulsion towards becoming a doctor. 'Is our family even made of humans? When I think of my future, I almost feel like a machine whose fate is already chosen,' her conclusion resulted in a major showdown between father and daughter. Dr Roy never imagined that his daughter would be foolish enough to not embrace a career that, according to him, practically every Indian aspires to.

'You are stupid to not see how easy it would be for you in life if you were to be a doctor. You just have to take my chair,' Dr Roy seemed clearly frustrated.

'Precisely the reason why I will never become a doctor,' Yogini replied, and rejected any further efforts by Dr Roy to convince her.

Although Dr Roy brought Yogini to the career counsellor at the repeated request of her school principal, he was trying his level best to convince the counsellor of the glories attached to a career in medicine, particularly for a person bearing the surname Roy. Meanwhile, the counsellor was insisting that Yogini was best suited to take a liberal arts course.

It was not that out of the two, Yogini sided with the counsellor. Rebel as she was, she detested the sixteen-personality test the counsellor had just asked her to undertake. Based on a series of objective questions, the test was to decide whether Yogini was an introvert or an extrovert, and whether she was more logical or more intuitive. For her, the sixteen-personality test questions were nothing but an attempt to box her into a specific personality type. Exactly what Yogini hated.

'Do you think that I am a machine?' Yogini's question had an immediate effect on the atmosphere of the room. The argument between her father and the counsellor instantly stopped.

Let us pause Yogini's story here and use our imagination for a moment.

Imagine that counsellor's chamber to be India. And imagine yourself, thousands of feet above the ground, sitting amidst the clouds and watching that room. Can you not see hundreds and hundreds of Dr Roys in that room convinced that every science student should pursue a career in medicine? And thousands and thousands of career counsellors dotted throughout the room, boxing the entire India into sixteen personalities and pushing them towards career fads? First selling medical and engineering colleges, then business schools and now liberal arts colleges? Can you not see millions of Indian children being forced into various queues to join others walking towards similar career paths? And thousands among them jumping one over the other to get inside the ironclad gates of a few prestigious colleges in few specific fields?

And amidst all this, can you hear Yogini's all-important question—

'Do you think that I am a machine?'

Perhaps, as only a few of the likes of Yogini in India currently show the courage to ask this question, and as we are thousands of feet above the ground, the all-important question remains inaudible. Only when the majority starts asking will this question become loud and clear, and force us to take corrective measures.

***

We all aspire to live in a house that comes with a brilliant view. Perhaps the otherwise harsh world looks far prettier from such a location. Often, like super successful Dr Roy, when we are comfortably residing in our little house enjoying a brilliant view of life, we tend to acquire a false sense of superiority towards our profession. And as a result, we often steer our children towards careers we consider superior.

But what happens if the whole country starts suffering from this anti-fluidity?

In the early 1990s, in the pre-globalisation era, the majority of meritorious India knew of only two career streams, medicine and engineering, hardly looking at the diverse spectrum of science-based careers; today, post-globalised India sees the vast majority of educated youth preparing for MBA entrance examinations.

Such an anti-fluid approach to education has hardly any room for a curious mind—its desire to tackle unexplored questions rather than gulp parroted solutions, its inquisitiveness to break out of a set mould.

Ironically, the higher one wants to aim in terms of the choice of colleges, the sooner one has to strip oneself of any wish to travel on unexplored knowledge paths, instead spending time perfecting standardised entrance examinations.

Learning is the most beautiful thing, yet the fear of failure in these examinations has mutated it into a torturous demon, which scares young minds away from the liberating fountains of knowledge.

All those who refuse to walk these set paths are ridiculed.

A change in subject streams and career line is seen as a sign of a fumbling mind. Study gaps and career gaps are dreadful words to appear in a CV.

To all those people who ridicule gaps in an educational journey, I urge them to learn from mathematician-philosopher René Descartes, who is regarded as the father of modern Western philosophy. Descartes—who famously wrote, 'I think, therefore I am'—once abandoned his education completely for the sake of travel.

We all would have read Shakespeare as part of our school curriculum, but no one tells us that when he was growing up, there were no professional theatres in London. Yet, Shakespeare went on to become a professional playwright, and as an astute businessman had the most successful theatre company in London, producing his own plays.

What was that quality that made William Shakespeare, the most famous English playwright in history, shine in a career that didn't even exist at the time of his birth?

Perhaps he realised the importance of being fluid early enough and refused to follow an established path. Perhaps for the same reason that Steve Jobs wanted to remain friends with both engineers and artists, Goethe never stopped at his literary career, and da Vinci kept experimenting with multiple fields.

A view from inside of our comfort zones threatens to turn us into machines. It takes away our ability to indulge in uncertainty and in turn infuses us with the tendency to mimic.

The more we mimic, the more machine-like we become.

I argue that the inquisitive, the explorers, the risk-takers are in a better position to face redundancy or unexpected turns in their career than those who use mimicking as a strategy.

I truly believe that in order to tackle the catastrophic arrival of the machines, the first key step is to eliminate the fear of

Dr Roy and other parents who are convinced that their children can only be successful by following their own career paths or those paths that seem to be riding the popularity wave.

Indeed, it is our fear, which convinces us that Yogini now has no future; that she has committed the biggest mistake of her life by refusing the safest career option currently available in India.

To know whether we are right or wrong, we need to look into the future of Yogini. But Yogini's story ends here. However, I know the story of an eighteenth-century doctor named Robert Darwin, whose personality appears quite similar to that of Dr Roy. And, as fate would have it, Dr Robert Darwin, too, had a child as rebellious as Yogini—who simply refused to step into his shoes to become a successful doctor.

Evolution Of A Rebellious Child

Born in the year 1766, Robert Darwin, an Englishman, received his medical degree from the University of Edinburgh, one of the best places to study medicine in those times.

And even before he turned twenty, Robert had earned his MD[1] from Leiden University, the oldest university of the Netherlands, and had set up his private medical practice in Shrewsbury, a quiet, hilly town, situated near the Welsh border in the UK.

With remarkable credentials for an eighteenth-century doctor, Dr Robert Darwin soon built a thriving medical practice, with patients coming to him from three nearby counties. Dr Robert Darwin was not only a good doctor, but also an astute real-estate investor. Utilising the small amount of money that he inherited from his mother's side, combined with his earnings, he became one of the biggest purchasers of property in Shrewsbury.

At one point in time, Dr Robert Darwin owned several buildings in Shrewsbury, which gave him a handsome monthly rental income.

Later in his life, Dr Robert Darwin was to become one of the wealthiest doctors in the world.[2]

With a wealth many times greater than that of Dr Roy's, Dr Robert Darwin, too, left no stone unturned to make his son a doctor.

But before we continue learning about Dr Robert Darwin's son, it is worth knowing about his father, Dr Erasmus Darwin, who, perhaps, can be considered even more famous than his son.

The Darwins were somewhat like our Roy family—a family committed to producing doctors. Dr Erasmus Darwin, who also earned his degree from Edinburgh Medical School, had two sons—Robert and Charles, both poised to become doctors. While Robert went on to become a successful doctor, Charles, the elder of the two, unfortunately died just before finishing his medical degree, apparently from septicaemia of a cut he experienced while performing an autopsy.

Dr Erasmus Darwin was so successful as a doctor that he once even refused an offer from King George III, then ruler of England, to become the royal physician.[3]

While Dr Robert Darwin didn't look much beyond the medical profession, his father had an amazing fluid spirit. Apart from being a doctor, he was a poet, an inventor, a philosopher and one of the champions of slavery abolishment and women's education. As an inventor, apart from proposing several interesting ideas, Dr Erasmus built an early version of the photocopier, a mechanical talking doll and a rudimentary rocket engine. However, he didn't patent any of these, fearing that it might damage his reputation as a doctor.

Perhaps Dr Erasmus Darwin's fluid soul drew inspiration from his friend Benjamin Franklin, one of the founding fathers of the USA who was not only a famous statesman, a successful author and a printer but also an inventor known for his contributions in the field of electricity and the invention of bifocal lenses.

There is one more important contribution of Dr Erasmus Darwin, perhaps his most important one, which we shall discuss later while unravelling the life of his grandson.

Dr Robert Darwin fathered two sons, one who quietly followed his father's and grandfather's footsteps and became a doctor, while the other one—like Yogini—turned rebel.

His name was Charles Darwin.

Yes, the same Charles Darwin whose theory of evolution can arguably be considered among the most profound scientific contributions ever made in human history.

Dr Robert, who named his son in the memory of his deceased brother—the one who couldn't complete his medical degree—may never have imagined that no Charles in their family was ever to become a doctor.

***

The legendary Charles Darwin was born on 12 February 1809 in Shrewsbury, which is also often referred to as the 'town of flowers'. Incidentally, the wealthiest doctor of his era, Dr Robert Darwin, knew the importance of a house with a view, as he built his residence[4] in Shrewsbury on 'The Mount',[5] a place on top of a hill overlooking a river. 'The Mount' was where the legendary Charles Darwin was born and spent his formative years.

Charles Darwin started assisting his doctor father as an intern as soon as he completed his schooling—his father wanted to give him a head start, as the young Charles had cleared the entrance exam and was soon to leave for Edinburgh Medical School.

However, contrary to Dr Robert Darwin's expectations, at the medical school, Charles found the lectures to be boring and often bunked his classes to spend time learning taxidermy.[6]

Incidentally, Charles had already shown signs of rebelliousness in school, where he demonstrated more fondness towards chemistry than towards animal science. He was so obsessed with chemistry that he had set up his own chemistry lab at home. His fondness for chemistry earned Charles Darwin the pet name 'gas' from his schoolmates!

Other than bunking regular medical classes, when he instead learned taxidermy, Charles Darwin spent considerable time in the company of one of his professors—Dr Grant.

Now is the time to throw light on the most important achievement of Charles Darwin's grandfather, Dr Erasmus. Not many outside the world of sciences know that Dr Erasmus Darwin—grandfather of Charles Darwin—proposed a rudimentary version of evolutionary theory.

Dr Erasmus Darwin proposed the idea that 'the strongest and most active animal should propagate the species',[7] which, although faulty and eventually corrected by his grandson Charles Darwin,[8] is considered the first time an evolutionary theory based on traits[9] came into being. Dr Erasmus proposed his views on evolution in *Zoonomia*, not so famous now but an influential book of those times.

Dr Grant, who was an MD but had already given up on medical practice to pursue his love for research on marine biology and invertebrate zoology, and was himself a towering botanist and anatomist of those times, was a great fan of Charles Darwin's grandfather and his *Zoonomia*. It was the company of Dr Grant that sowed the seeds of love for evolutionary science in Charles Darwin.

The news that his son Charles was bunking classes and spending time in the company of Dr Grant did not go down well with Dr Robert Darwin. He immediately took him out of

Edinburgh Medical School and enrolled him in the University of Cambridge to study a Bachelor of Arts.

It wasn't that Dr Robert Darwin had any love for the study of arts. This was his idea of giving a stable career to his son. In those days, a minister with the Church of England enjoyed a prestigious position in society, for which graduation was a necessary requirement. After failing at his plan A—make his son a doctor—Dr Robert Darwin had already started working on plan B—get his son a prestigious degree, buy him some land in a village to establish a church and marry him into a rich family.

However, just as Yogini did not have any intention of following Dr Roy's plans, Charles too did not spend his time in Cambridge by the book.

While most of the students spent their evenings in the pub, Charles Darwin was found attending discussions on natural history. Charles's cousin, named Fox, who was also at Cambridge, introduced him to the *bad* habit of collecting beetles of all kinds and shapes. Not stopping at collecting all kinds of insects, Charles Darwin also spent time learning geology at Cambridge.

Charles Darwin's activities at Cambridge did not please his father one bit, and the senior Darwin eventually called him 'a rat catcher' and 'a disgrace to the family'.[10]

It was in 1831, at the age of twenty-two, that Charles Darwin got the opportunity to sail on a multi-year expedition to conduct a geological survey of the world. His father initially objected to this expedition, considering it a waste of time, but eventually reluctantly agreed to fund his son's historic journey. The expedition lasted for over five years, during which Charles Darwin collected those most important specimens that he later used as evidence to build his groundbreaking theory of evolution.

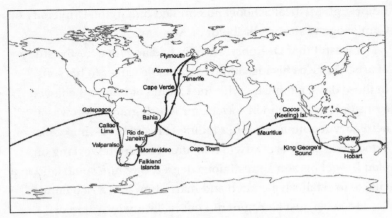

The Voyage of Charles Darwin, 1831-1836

Interestingly, while researching the Darwins, I realised that the learning approaches of the grandfather, son and grandson could be deciphered through the metaphor of an hourglass. That is, while Dr Robert Darwin had a narrow knowledge base, both his father, Dr Erasmus Darwin and his son, Charles Darwin, not only crossed over into several fields but were also more sensitive towards the sociocultural upheavals of those times.

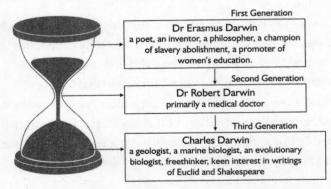

First Generation
Dr Erasmus Darwin
a poet, an inventor, a philosopher, a champion of slavery abolishment, a promoter of women's education.

Second Generation
Dr Robert Darwin
primarily a medical doctor

Third Generation
Charles Darwin
a geologist, a marine biologist, an evolutionary biologist, freethinker, keen interest in writings of Euclid and Shakespeare

Hourglass learning approach in the three generation of Darwins

One key ingredient that seems to have contributed to the achievements of the legendary Charles Darwin was his refusal to walk on a predetermined path—it is not likely that Charles Darwin started his life thinking he would one day change the way our species looks at its origin.

We may all point to different reasons for his success, but for me it was definitely Darwin's willingness to absorb from various fields that evolved his thinking.

For example, Darwin was in Chile when he experienced an earthquake and found that the rocks on the seashore, which had embedded marine shells, were now slightly raised above the sea water level. When he travelled inland from the seashore, it was Darwin's background in geology that helped him to observe that such a rising of the earth level was happening in that area over several centuries and that life was adapting to these environmental changes.

Similarly, after returning from his voyage, Darwin spent time in the company of his freethinking[11] brother in London, where he got to know about Thomas Robert Malthus' now famous essay on the 'principle of population' (not from the field of biology but welfare economics).

According to the essay, if unchecked, the human population would double every twenty-five years and would soon surpass the available food supply. In his autobiography, Darwin (pp 119-121) mentions the contribution of the essay to his theory of the 'origin of species by means of natural selection':

> In October 1838, that is, fifteen months after I had begun my systematic enquiry, I happened to read for amusement Malthus on Population, and being well prepared to appreciate the struggle for existence which everywhere goes on from long-continued observation of the habits of animals and plants, it at once struck me that under these circumstances favourable variations would tend to be preserved, and unfavourable ones to be destroyed. The result of this would be the formation of new species. Here, then, I had at last got a theory by which to work.[12]

Although he followed an unusual educational path, Charles Darwin successfully resisted societal pressures and eventually utilised his education to reach a destination that many can only aspire to.

In fact, every education policymaker of India would dream of copying a learning environment, a curriculum or a mechanism that could produce the likes of Charles Darwin. But then our fluid Darwin was a rat-catcher, an insect-gatherer, a medical-degree dropout, a graduate in arts—who took inspiration from artist-scientist Goethe—who in spite of working on evolutionary biology loved reading Euclid and Shakespeare, and in spite of having a brilliant mind was happy to work towards an uncertain career destination.

How does one copy that?

Lessons On Artificial Intelligence From A Nineteenth-century Storyteller

The arrival of intelligent machines clearly spells that whether we are a Dr Roy or a Dr Robert Darwin, no one is safe in the future.

Before we further explore the threat of the ones artificially intelligent, let me share with you a small anecdote from my childhood.

I was around thirteen when our school opened its first computer lab. In those days, visiting the school computer lab was almost like visiting a shrine. The expensive PCs were veiled under individual tablecloths in the dust-free room and were only to be touched under adult supervision. The computer lab was the only air-conditioned and carpeted classroom, which we couldn't enter without taking off our shoes.

As an honest confession, I couldn't get my head around the early lessons on programming. With both of my parents working as medical doctors, I was poised to become a doctor myself and hence at that time did not see much of a use in learning a computer language. Thus, I deployed my usual tested technique of cramming to clear my school computer exams.

However, I was fascinated by the capabilities of computers.

Incidentally, my close friends in school comprised a diverse group with interests ranging from physics to biology to acting to dancing. We loved spending hours discussing things, but these all had to be outside our taught curriculum.

It was some day in July, raining cats and dogs, and a bunch of my friends and I were holed up in one of our friend's rooms discussing our usual stuff, when I turned the conversation towards something that my mind had been toying over for a long time.

'The computer is able to calculate $2 + 2 = 4$ or guess that the capital of India is Delhi, because we have already input the correct result. Right? So basically, a computer is nothing but a library with the right answers.' Although I had no clue about how to write such a code or what went inside a machine language, I still pretended I was an expert in computer programming.

Thanks to my doctor parents, by the time I was thirteen I was aware of the all-important term 'neuron', from the human nervous system, and the cell's capability of processing and transferring information. My father, apart from being a paediatrician, also spared time to teach me (and my sister) the foundation subjects required to study medicine.

Thus, I combined the two worlds of computers and human anatomy and continued my speech, 'You see, our brain works just like a computer. Just that it has a code written with millions of permutations and combinations, which gives it the intelligence to say or do the right thing at the right time. Like these millions of neurons,' I pointed to my brain and pretended to be an expert on neuroscience.

'Now imagine if we were to write such a code for a computer

by giving it a library of each and every probable eventuality, telling it to react and act in the most appropriate manner. Would it not be like creating an artificial brain?' I expected to enthral my friends but nothing of the sort happened.

One of the friends, who was perhaps the best among us with computers, replied, showing no excitement whatsoever, 'You know how much time it takes to write a code just to calculate 2 + 2? Now imagine the time it will take to write a code that would make a computer an expert on mathematics alone. Now add the time for coding the knowledge from all the possible subjects. It is not humanly possible.'

Staring at defeat, I quickly changed the topic, but the thought lingered in my head for a very long time.

Although my thoughts on creating an artificial brain were quite immature, little did I realise that I had som ow stumbled upon the world of artificial intelligence.

There are many sophisticated definitions of the term, but in the simplest sense, the closer a machine gets to mimicking a human, the more intelligent it can be considered on the scale of artificial intelligence.

Expanding the above simple definition, we may see artificial intelligence from the perspective of four broad categories:

1. Dexterity: the ability of a machine to use its robotic parts (especially fingers) as humans would use them (with the same reflex capability and finesse). For example, performing microsurgeries, assembling, drawing, writing, painting, climbing, catching, etc.
2. Subject intelligence: a machine's grasp of existing knowledge and, in turn, its application (by and large, reproduction of existing ideas and capabilities). For example, the diagnostic and analytical capabilities of Dr Watson and Mr Ross.

3. Creative intelligence: the ability of a machine to use existing knowledge and create something new, furthering the frontiers of knowledge. For example, research, problem-solving, innovation, new design, self-written programmes, self-composed songs, performance in unexpected situations, etc.

4. Social and emotional intelligence: the ability of a machine to behave and act as a social animal. For example, friendliness, relationships, interactions, compassion, caring, feelings, etc.

Although it is headed in the right direction, this simple definition immediately opens a Pandora's box, as we humans are still debating what can be considered the right mix of intelligence even for ourselves. For example, should a robot be a socialist or should it be a capitalist? And if a robot is a country's president or prime minister and happens to be a follower of Mahatma Gandhi, should it invest in defence? Should a robot be an extrovert or an introvert? Making it even more complex: should a robot know how and when to lie?

So, do we know the right answers to these questions?

Because obviously the answer to what machines can do—or at least what humans would allow machines to do—is fundamental. This is important, as it will eventually decide which jobs will be safe in the future and the skill set required in doing those jobs.

As many of you may know, Facebook founder Mark Zuckerberg and technology celebrity and CEO of Tesla cars Elon Musk got into a public spat. It wasn't fisticuffs, yet it caused a major storm in technology circuits. Musk, an avid technology investor, is known for considering progress in artificial intelligence as 'the greatest risk we face as a civilisation'.[1] He is clear that, if kept unchecked, machines will go beyond mere job snatching and almost take humans to an apocalyptic end.

However, the Facebook founder doesn't agree with Musk on the dangers of machines. Zuckerberg, in a recent live chat, when asked to react to such views considered them to be 'pretty irresponsible':

> I think people who are naysayers and try to drum up these doomsday scenarios [referring to Elon Musk]—I just, I don't understand it. It's really negative and in some ways I actually think it is pretty irresponsible.[2]

Musk shot back by asserting that Zuckerberg's 'understanding of the subject is limited'.[3]

Although, in this argument, I personally lean towards Musk, the verbal fight between Zuckerberg and Musk clearly suggests that a lot of uncertainty persists around the impact of machines.

So, how does one prepare for the future?

Our question becomes even tougher when we dig deeper into the various studies, which offer us different answers. Let's take the example of the Oxford study, which examined 702 jobs and predicted that 47 per cent of them were 'at risk'.[4] For the curious ones, the BBC website, drawing on the Oxford study, has even started a section titled, 'Will a robot take your job?' with a search box that allows you to just type in your job category. The website immediately spells out the precise percentage of risk that a particular job carries.

While the results from the study may be helpful to introduce us to the threats of automation, they also carry the risk of misdirecting us towards following a herd mentality. For example, the study suggests that a psychologist will face just a 0.7 per cent risk, while a chartered accountant is considered to be at a 95 per cent risk. Considering that it only carries a 0.7 per cent risk, a lot of us may want to become psychologists and drop the idea of taking up chartered accountancy altogether.

But then, is it not important to ask whether a poorly-skilled psychologist has a higher risk of losing his or her job when compared to a better-skilled chartered accountant?

In fact, even if we were to assume that there would be no jobs in chartered accountancy, the chances to switch careers of a better-skilled chartered accountant are far greater than those of a poorly-skilled psychologist.

This is crucial because the World Economic Forum forecasts that a person, no matter what his profession, would have to acquire at least 35 per cent of newer skills if he were to save his career.

Therefore, while Zuckerberg may disagree with Musk on the catastrophic impact of machines, he will have to agree that future workers will certainly need to be more adaptable, willing to acquire new skills and prepared to work in multiple fields.

That is, the future will belong to those who are fluid—like Charles Darwin who got bored by the idea of doing mundane things and wanted to explore new areas, despite all ordeals— like Yogini who refused to be treated as if she couldn't think for herself—or like all those people who refuse to walk on predictable paths and hence prevent themselves from turning into machines.

Importantly, while the field of artificial intelligence may still be at a nascent stage, one thing looks quite certain: the closer humans remain to the abilities of a machine, the more they are at risk of losing their livelihoods to a machine.[5] For example, Martin Ford, in his book *Rise of the Robots: Technology and the Threat of a Jobless Future* (2015) asserts that the jobs at highest risk are the ones that are 'on some level routine, repetitive and predictable'.

I expanded this conclusion and conceptualised a 'rudimentary scale of intelligence'. That is, as demonstrated in the illustration below, if being more similar to machines increases the risk of redundancy for us, then the further we are from being a machine, the more equipped we are to lead ourselves into the future with less risk.

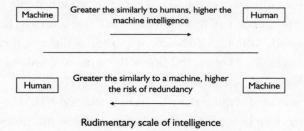

Rudimentary scale of intelligence

As per the principles of this scale, I argue that a fluid person will have more chances to move away from the machine and be more human-like, because of his exploratory nature, diverse exposure to various fields, reluctance to do repetitive and routine work and never-ending desire to challenge the defined boundaries.

I want to emphasise that AI thrives on anti-fluidity. Here, I would like to bring Mark Zuckerberg back into the discussion. Facebook may have started with an innocent agenda but, to me, there is no doubt that it is has now become quite dangerous as far as the world of thinking and learning goes.

Facebook and other similar platforms continuously spy on our activities and interests and create algorithms which ape our clicks and dish us similar kind of stuff. It is less work for them if they box and keep us predictable. If one is not careful, it is easy to get trapped inside a bubble where we assume that we are being exposed to balanced news and views, whereas in reality we are just consuming what the algorithms want us to. And this becomes a vicious cycle. Clearly, we need to safeguard ourselves from such platforms, as the more predictable we would become, the more we will lose to AI.

***

Have you ever noticed that it often so happens that most of the fortune telling about how our future will shape up is done by people belonging to the STEM camp? Even the media and the general public pay more attention to those with a STEM background. Although Zuckerberg and Musk differ in their perspectives, they both stand under the same umbrella of technology.

However, it is quite risky to exclude the non-STEM perspective on how to shape our future, because machines are not the only impactful factor[6]; our world is also changing on the social, cultural, political and economic levels.

For example, the dawn of globalisation and privatisation has already created and destroyed many business ventures. Movements such as Occupy Wall Street already reflect the pressure on the current form of capitalism to be better equipped for fair distribution of wealth. Further, a few decades back, climate change was hardly an issue, whereas today and in the future, a large number of people are needed to work on strategies, technologies, policies, etc. to protect and preserve mother Earth. Similarly, the rise of social media requires experts in human b aviour and preferences. With easier access to knowledge, discussions are already underway on the future of universities and schools.

There are many examples like the ones above, which signify that technology is not the only influencing factor in the future of our civilisation and hence, incorporating variables from diverse fields, i.e., being fluid becomes almost mandatory. What I mean to say is that it is quite important to understand that the difference between Musk and Zuckerberg on the impact of artificial intelligence cannot be resolved unless we look at it beyond the lens of technology and bring in perspectives from fields ranging from evolutionary biology to sociology to philosophy to economics to education to music to history to politics to dance to spirituality.

The changes occurring in diverse fields compel us to realise that artificial intelligence cannot be perfected only by confining ourselves to the womb of a technology bubble, but by breaking subject boundaries to gather from sociocultural–political–economic perspectives.

Such a view is all the more important, as many scholars believe that the future will require a large number of experts on artificial intelligence. For example, the Zhejiang Province in China aims to hire around 100,000 AI professionals in the next five years.[7] Almost all big companies in the world are investing heavily in AI. Andrew Ng, a leading expert on artificial intelligence, calls for the preparation of more than a million AI professionals.[8] Such professionals must embrace the fluid approach, moving beyond mere technology expertise, in order to be effective in the dynamic future.

There should be no shame in accepting that it is literally impossible to forecast what kind of a future is in store for us. It does not exist today and people are just trying hard to make the best possible bet.

So who out of Musk and Zuckerberg will win the battle of forecasting?

I say he will be the one who is more fluid. The one who doesn't see the world only through the eyes of technology. The one who has crossed more subject boundaries and is willing to absorb from as many diverse fields as possible. Because I can tell you of one such person who did not belong to the world of technology yet came closer to being the most accurate future teller of human advancement.

***

We can all be better prepared for the dynamic future if we learn from the legendary science fiction storyteller, HG Wells.

You might very well laugh at my attempt to create an artificial brain, but you certainly cannot laugh at what HG Wells thought almost eighty years ago. The 'world brain', as Wells termed it, was an idea that carried the seeds of the World Wide Web, Google search engine and Wikipedia, all in one go.

And this was decades before the world saw any of these advancements.

Wells was born on 21 September 1866, in Kent, about 16 kilometres from central London—at a time long before the birth of computers and when barely any homes in England had electricity.

Before we understand Wells' idea of the world brain, we need to reflect on what exactly an encyclopaedia is. If we, as humans, ever create an artificial brain that can hold each and every piece of knowledge available, and if we try plotting a timeline of its progress,[9] an encyclopaedia should come at point zero.

Encyclopaedias	Online search engines	Artificial brain
	1993	

Timeline in terms of storing, searching and retrieving capabilities

Before online search engines became the kind of go-to source where all information is available, it was the job of an encyclopaedia to provide authentic information at one place. If one were to follow the history of the encyclopaedia, it could be considered an attempt to create a single, legitimate, definitional source of knowledge.

But the entries of an encyclopaedia were in the hands of a small body of scholars, and had no room for dispute and disagreement by its readers.

In fact, the idea for Wikipedia came into being to tackle exactly this weakness.

The entries on Wikipedia are created, edited and monitored by a large number of volunteers, and allow the provision of endless revisions.

But there were only encyclopaedias and no Wikipedia when HG Wells lived. And Wells knew that encyclopaedias, available only in the form of printed books, with no capacity for readers to talk back, are limited in their capabilities. In a lecture delivered in the US in 1937, while presenting the idea of a world brain, Wells said:

> ...our contemporary encyclopaedias are still in the coach-and-horses phase of development, rather than in the phase of the automobile and the aeroplane...our world is changing...but it is not developing the brain and the sensitiveness and delicacy necessary for its new life.[10]

Like the modern-day Wikipedia, the 'world brain' of Wells was to be in the 'form of a network', 'alive and growing and changing continually, under revision, extension and replacement' and in 'continual correspondence with every university, every research institution...every survey, every statistical bureau in the world'. It was to be, 'the mental background of every intelligent man in the world' and to be brought in contact with 'every fresh mind'.

The world brain was an idea much ahead of its time.

But then, the world brain was not the only path-breaking thought of HG Wells, who is considered to be the father of science fiction writing. To claim that he created the genre may not be an overstatement.

Through his novels, Wells attempted to show how the world might change over the next hundreds or even thousands of years.

And if he were to be right, he would require incredible imagination and ability to predict, and a sophisticated understanding of all kinds of forces operating in the world.

And boy was he right!

Wells introduced the idea of man walking on the moon in his novel, *The First Men in the Moon* (1901), almost sixty-eight years before it actually happened. Dr Cavor, the protagonist scientist in the book, creates a futuristic spacecraft that uses a shield layered with anti-gravity material around its hull to escape Earth's gravity.

In his 1899 novel, *When the Sleeper Wakes*, people travelled between cities on a 300-feet-wide, automatic, movable highway, an expanded version of the modern-day travellator that ran on a giant conveyer belt. Wells' movable highway was not a simple road, but was fitted with cushioned seats and refreshment kiosks.

Wells thought of automatic sliding doors almost fifty years before they came into existence!

In the world created by HG Wells, people wore wireless wrist intercoms like our current smart wristwatches, exchanged voice messages and video-chatted over phones.

The imagination of HG Wells was so powerful that almost all sci-fi Hollywood films, whether they depict alien invasion, interplanetary war or time travel, would certainly find some of their roots in his work.

In fact, the term 'time machine' was coined by none other than HG Wells.[11]

The Hollywood super-hit film *Hollow Man*, which was released in the year 2000 and grossed over US$ 190 million[12] is based on the novel *The Invisible Man* by Wells, written almost 100 years before the film captured the imagination of a worldwide audience.

Here, an important question to ask is, how is it that the worlds created by Wells are still relevant? Often when people write on HG Wells, they highlight his uncanny ability to predict technological advancements. However, the true power of Wells was his ability to bring in other perspectives, such as sociocultural, political and economic, while creating his world.

For example, almost three decades before the atomic bomb came into existence, Wells described uranium-based bombs being dropped from aeroplanes in his book, *The World Set Free* (1913). However, it wasn't just the idea of the atomic bomb—he also laid out the dire consequences of such inventions for human life. Leo Szilard, the Hungarian physicist who conceived the nuclear chain reaction and patented the idea of a nuclear reactor, claimed that the book inspired him to contemplate 'what the liberation of atomic energy on a large scale would mean',[13] forcing him to not make his patents public, as the book had shown how big cities can be destroyed in minutes.

In *The Shape of Things to Come* (1933), Wells prophetically predicted that a world war would break out within a few years, starting in eastern Europe before involving all other nations. In the climax of his book, the key powers form a world government to avoid such conflicts. We may not have seen a world government, but the formation of international organisations such as the United Nations, International Monetary Fund and World Bank was partly inspired by the work of HG Wells. In fact, as soon as World War II ended, Wells started writing letters to *The Times* newspaper, highlighting his ideas on human rights. His ideas were formally used in the foundation documents of the United Nations.

If one looks at the preparatory days of HG Wells, one cannot fail to notice his willingness to absorb information from all subject areas. Unlike several key authors of his era, Wells was born into a poor family, which introduced him to the harsh realities of the class disparities prevalent in English society in those days.

His father and mother ran a small shop, but the earnings fell short; hence, the father played professional cricket for the Kent county team to make ends meet.

Wells broke his leg at the age of seven and hence had to spend most of his time in bed, reading books borrowed from the local library. This was when he was introduced to the works of Plato. His creation, *The Invisible Man*, must have gained some inspiration from Plato's idea of the ring of Gyges, which carried magical powers and could turn its owner invisible at will.

During his teens, Wells had to work as a draper selling clothes in a shop, which inspired him to conceive similar characters in his novels *The Wheels of Chance* and *Kipps: The Story of a Simple Soul*, through which he mocked the disparity in wealth distribution that existed in society.

Wells was not a technocrat but a biologist by education. Thanks to a scholarship, he studied the subject under the famous biologist TH Huxley, who happened to be a close acquaintance of Charles Darwin and an ardent propagator of his theory of evolution, so much so that Huxley was often called 'Darwin's Bulldog'. His training under Huxley had a deep impact on Wells, and the worlds he sewed, whether those of humans or aliens, often used the threads of evolution, genetics, survival of the fittest and social Darwinism. A remarkable display is seen in *The Island of Dr Moreau* (1896), in which the absconding doctor uses genetic engineering to carry out his experiments, transforming animals into humans.

Although trained in biology, Wells was an avid reader of sociology, philosophy, economics, religion and technology.

His understanding of various subjects is brilliantly displayed in his dystopian novel *The War of the Worlds* (1898), which almost a century later was turned into a Hollywood blockbuster starring Tom Cruise and directed by Steven Spielberg.[14] The book revolves around the invasion of southern England by technologically superior Martians. As an older species, the Martians have evolved to be more intelligent but less compassionate than humans. The Martians kill humans with the aim of capturing Earth, demonstrating their colonial attributes. The almost-destroyed Earth of the later chapters displays how a dystopian world might look if it were to face a technological war, acting almost like a warning for our civilisation.

HG Wells truly understood the importance of breaking subject boundaries for the advancement of human civilisation. In order to present a coherent picture of the world, Wells wrote *The Outline of History: The Whole Story of Man* (1919), which became one of the most popular books of its time. The reason for him undertaking this project was truly his fluid spirit, as rightly reflected in his own words (1938):

> And that is why I have spent a few score thousand hours of my particular allotment of vitality in making outlines of history, short histories of the world, general accounts of the science of life, attempts to bring economic, financial and social life into one conspectus and even, still more desperate, struggles to estimate the possible consequences of this or that set of operating causes upon the future of mankind.[15]

If we reflect on the words of HG Wells and combine them with the deep impact of machines on the future of mankind, it becomes even clearer that we have to be as fluid as possible—to enhance our imagination and our ability to compr end the changes expected in the future workplace.

In order to further confirm the utility of the fluid approach, let's gather lessons from HG Wells and apply them to a troubled workplace we know from present times—the dying Pigeon, our fictional start-up.

Firstly, the success of HG Wells tells us that Fatima—the first employee of Pigeon—was not doing such a bad thing by submerging herself in the world of science fiction. Fatima's exposure to the sci-fi genre fuelled her imagination, which in turn enabled her to turn around a presentation on the future of hologram technology in mobile phones in just one night.

In fact, Pigeon might have been saved if Rahul and Priya had recognised Fatima's imaginative powers, ability to research and comfort with deciphering a new area, and treated her as a valuable part of the start-up instead of a stereotypical computer programmer.

It may not be surprising that, if Fatima keeps on developing her imagination by learning from other areas, she may surpass Rahul and Priya in establishing a successful high-tech start-up and excelling in the machine-filled future.

Incidentally, at Pigeon, Rahul and Priya may not have noticed Fatima's potential, but Mr Sheshadri, their investor, definitely took notice. We can only attribute this to Mr Sheshadri's fluid outlook, which made him encourage Fatima to speak her mind in that fateful meeting. Like HG Wells, Mr Sheshadri, too, lived a life beyond that of a mere technical entrepreneur. His concerns for the ill effects of mobile technology and his contribution to modernisation of his native village are both an indication of his understanding of sociopolitical–cultural landscapes.

Indeed, Mr Sheshadri's approach can be considered almost opposite to that of Rahul's father, who received a large chunk of his revenue from sand mining. If Rahul's father hadn't created a little prison around his idea of business he would have had an understanding of the ecological impact of such activities.

And this would have helped him to quickly recognise that such businesses would soon face extinction.[16]

The teachings of HG Wells again bring the spotlight back onto the way we currently educate ourselves.

After all, how many educational institutions and AI experts can we find who would be fluid enough to include the views and ideas of a nineteenth-century storyteller in a curriculum devised to understand the threat of machines?

But,
I Am A Specialist,
My Friend

Like A Two-faced Snake, Our Two-faced Education

We have already reached that stage where one is considered educated only if he or she is a specialist. The consequences of not being a specialist are pierced continuously into the hearts and minds of the younger generation.

'What do you want to be?' As soon as a child gathers its senses, this question starts chasing them like a missile locked on to its target. Often, the pressure compels the parent or the child to choose a specialist label so they can feel safe under its shadow (doctor, engineer, MBA, etc.). And once the label is chosen, everything that weakens the glue of this label is considered a waste of time.

So, how do we currently prepare specialists in India?

Those who understand the Indian schooling system are well aware of its 'double-faced', two-track nature.

With the aim of becoming an expert, every student rushes on two tracks simultaneously—one that is visible, existing under the bright sky with fresh air but the other one is hidden—existing right beneath this visible path in the form of a dark, deep and lonely tunnel.

The visible track—Track 1—is what is evident to all:

Go to school—attend classes—clear exams.

We are told that this visible track has no relation with becoming an expert. Actually it is the dark, dingy hidden track—Track 2—which leads us to become a specialist. The one on which a student walks alone, away from the apparent eyes of society:

Attend coaching classes—prepare for the college entrance—once cleared, start preparing for the next entrance.

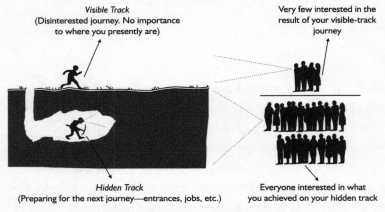

The two-faced nature of the Indian education system

Sadly, the current situation has become such that by and large we all have little interest in what a child achieves under that clear sky breathing fresh air. Our eyes only remain focused on the exits of these dark tunnels where the majority remain buried and only a few lucky ones are able to emerge out successfully.

With each passing year, this dark tunnel is becoming longer and longer. Previously, a school student only had to start preparing for entrances in class XII, but now the competition demands that a young child should pick the shovel even while he or she is in just class IX or VIII.

If we think that we are free from the clutches of this two-headed snake after our school life, we are wrong. For those in college, the weight of shovel increases as one has to start preparing for a postgraduate entrance. And for those aiming for super-specialisation, the trend continues.

Here I would like to share an incident from my school life, when I happened to get a good scolding from one of my beloved school friends.

We both were in class XII and preparing for the medical entrance exam. As demanded by the two-faced education, the top-ranked students in our school had virtually given up on all extracurricular activities. School was only attended to achieve the minimum attendance, and the syllabus was learned only to clear the school examinations. Our entire attention was focused on attending coaching classes and learning the tricks for clearing objective-type questions.

Incidentally, I used to be the school head boy and quite an active participant in extracurricular activities. And although I too attended the coaching classes, I often wasted my time discussing unrelated things, like artificial brains, etc.

My dear friend always got irritated when he found out that I had spent my valuable time on such a discussion. He cared for me and feared that I would fail the medical entrance exam due to all these distractions.

It was a day after one of those evenings of discussion. Our zoology coaching class had just ended and we stood on the street near our mopeds, ready to leave.

I committed the mistake of divulging to him about my discussion on French Revolution the previous evening. It was enough to bring out the simmering anger in him. He blasted me when I told him of my conversation. 'In spite of me warning you several times, you do not listen. You surely do not want to pass the entrance!'

'Well, we also spent some time discussing electrons and protons,' I tried calming him down.

'Do you seriously think that all these discussions will get you more marks in the physics paper? And explain, how will physics help you to become a specialist doctor?'

My explanations failed to have any effect. He went ahead and spilled his anger at the fact that I was even participating in the annual school play! It was almost criminal for someone aiming to clear the entrances to be involved in any extracurricular activity.

'Once you lose this chance, you will never get it back. But I guess you don't realise. Just think about your parents. You are surely playing with your future!' he declared, and left without waiting for my reply.

My friend truly understood the degree of discipline and strength required to work in the dark tunnel. He knew that the shovel couldn't rest if one needs to emerge out in the stipulated time. Hence, he not only successfully cleared the entrance but subsequent entrances to become a specialist doctor.

I, the first-rank holder of my school, the one always interested in discussing, dancing and acting, threw my shovel and refused to dig any further and in the process failed the medical entrance.

The hidden track was proved victorious then and continues to do so, as even after a couple of decades, millions of students in India, remain hidden away from our eyes in these dark tunnels with moving shovels in their tired hands in the hope of becoming specialists and super-specialists.

The Pain Of A World-class Specialist

In 1932, a boy was born in a tiny, sleepy village of the southernmost Indian state, Kerala. Not many would have predicted that the boy would go on to become the most revered infrastructure specialist of our times. His village was located in a serene region surrounded by mountains, beautiful rivers and dense forests, and was also less than 100 kilometres from the shores of the Arabian Sea. Perhaps the juxtaposition of such varied landscape features gave him the confidence to execute infrastructure projects with ease, whether they were over water, through tough terrain or under the soil.

In 1964, when the boy was just over thirty, a powerful cyclone struck the Sri Lankan and Tamil Nadu regions, resulting in the loss of hundreds of lives and severe damage to property.

Pamban Bridge, India's first and longest sea-link railway bridge, which connects the island city of Rameshwaram to mainland India, was also severely damaged.

The bridge was the only connecting surface link, and its

quick repair was crucial for thousands of lives stranded on the island. The boy, who was now an engineer, was put in charge of bringing the 2-kilometre-long Pamban Bridge back to its feet, with a deadline of ninety days. Fully understanding that each passing day was critical for human lives, the boy completed the task in a record forty-six days.

In 1970, from the extreme southern part of India, the boy travelled to the east and reached Kolkata, where he headed the first metro rail project of India.

In 1979, the boy was again summoned to the South to pull the troubled Cochin (now Kochi) ship-building yard out of crisis. The shipyard had been struggling for several years to build its first ship. Within two years, the boy turned the fortunes of the place around and helped the shipyard to launch its first ship.

In 1990, the boy, now on the verge of retiring, was called again to spearhead a 750-kilometre-long railway track, to be laid through one of the most difficult terrains of the world. The track was to connect the south-western coastal belt of India, which had always been a challenge due to the presence of the humongous Western Ghats mountain range. In the path of this track were steep valleys, deep rivers, rocky peaks and many patches of dense forest, which required the building of over 2,000 bridges and 91 tunnels for the successful completion of the project. The boy again showed his excellence as an infrastructure specialist and completed the task within the specified timeline and budget, overcoming landslides, heavy rains and even the Gulf oil crises,[1] which saw several projects of the world stalled due to the steep rise in oil prices.

Konkan Railways, as the track came to be known, took over eight years to complete and is considered to be one of the most challenging railway projects in the world.

The boy was destined to leave his imprints all across India and hence, in 1997, he was called to head the ambitious Delhi metro project. There was a lot of scepticism regarding the viability of the metro rail link in Delhi, with many fearing that the project would overshoot its deadline and budget. However, the boy again proved all the sceptics wrong and successfully completed the Delhi metro project, which eventually laid the path for several other Indian cities to undertake metro projects of similar magnitude.

It was the success of the Delhi metro that earned our specialist boy the title of 'Metro Man'.

However, the topmost infrastructure specialist of India is not a happy man—specifically, when his eyes are searching for specialists of his kind among the younger generation.

In one of his recent interviews,[2] E Sreedharan, our beloved Metro Man, described the quality of the majority of India's engineers as 'below acceptable standards'. E Sreedharan pondered the slow pace of the installation of metro rail networks in India and blamed it primarily on the lack of high-quality specialists. In fact, he suggested that whatever small number of metro-rail specialists India produces, they get 'poached' from one project to another with outrageous salary jumps.

The story of our world-class specialist boy leaves us with a very painful question—

Why, in spite of almost the whole of India walking inside the hidden tunnels, our Metro Man is not able to find even a handful of infrastructure specialists?

***

When the Metro Man, E Sreedharan, was born (in the year 1932, in pre-Independence India), there were only seventeen

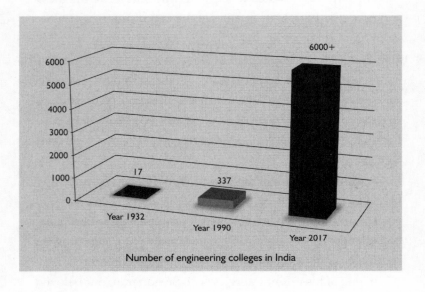

Number of engineering colleges in India

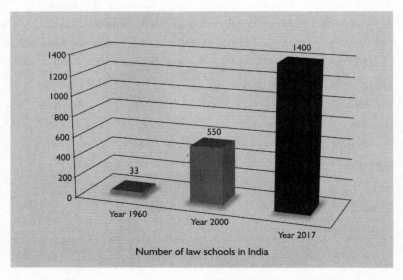

Number of law schools in India

Post 1990 spurt in the total number of colleges in India in various disciplines

engineering colleges across the whole country. The number did not even exceed fifty when he graduated from a local government engineering college.

Similar to engineering, the other disciplines also faced a shortage of the universities and colleges required to educate the growing Indian population. For example, for a total population of 44.95 crore (449.5 million) in 1960,[3] India only had thirty-three law colleges, ten management institutes and eighty-six medical colleges.[4]

Once the Indian economy opened its doors to the world in the early 1990s, the demand for a large workforce seemed quite natural. With the rationale to fuel the growing economy, the government opened up the higher education sector to private Indian players.

This step ballooned the number of degree colleges in India in a most unchecked fashion.

For example, in 1990, India had 337 engineering colleges. But by 2006, sixteen years later, this number had multiplied by five, with the total number of colleges standing at 1511. Thus, in this one-and-a-half decade between 1990 and 2006, every year almost eighty engineering colleges opened in India.

If this seems like reckless speed, just notice what happened in the next two years. By 2008, India had 2388 engineering colleges, which means that, between 2006 and 2008, on average, every day one engineering college was getting an approval!

But then, nobody seemed to notice the folly and the trend continued.

With another 2000 odd engineering colleges opening in India from 2008 to 2014, the number of engineering colleges doubled in a period of six years.

Currently, as I write, the number of engineering colleges in

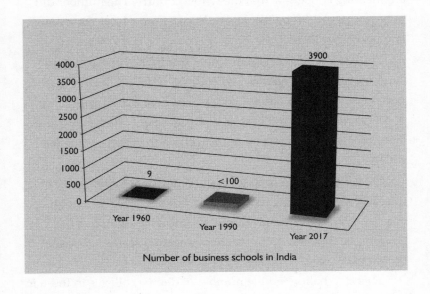

Number of business schools in India

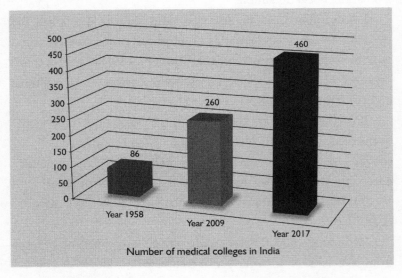

Number of medical colleges in India

Post 1990 spurt in the total number of colleges in India in various disciplines

India stands at around 6000, creating around 1.5 million (15 lac) engineers annually.

This senseless growth spurt was not restricted to engineering alone. Today, India has around 3500 business schools (from fewer than 100 in 1992), around 1400 law colleges[5] and 460 medical colleges.[6]

As astonishing as it may sound, due to the bloated growth in the number of colleges opening in India over the past three decades, whether it is engineering, law, medicine or business, India beats every other nation in the world in number of colleges per country.

However, the higher the graph of quantity of colleges went, the deeper the quality of Indian higher education settled into the pits of mediocrity. As an unfortunate result, in the past several years, not a single Indian university has made it into even the top 200 universities of the world.[7]

On a cumulative level, India produces 7.8 million (78 lac) graduates every year, the most in the world.[8]

Logically, one would believe that the exponential rise in the number of colleges would increase the size of the skilled workforce being sent to the marketplace; however, the free rein given to the mushrooming colleges shatters any such dreams of ours as a nation.

In a recent survey (2016), worryingly, nine out of ten engineering and MBA graduates in India were found to be unemployable.[9]

The results of such surveys are confirmed by our Metro Man's observations. According to E Sreedharan, India suffers from a severe shortage of metro-rail specialists, yet he doesn't think that these can be produced, even in the 6000-odd private engineering colleges:

I am not very enthusiastic. In fact, some private colleges have already approached us [to start a course on metro rail]. Private college means it becomes a business. Education cannot be taken as a business. They want to start the course not to help the metros or the nation, but find a business opportunity and charge high fees.[10]

Sadly, it is not only the fields of engineering or management—the performance of our specialists is brought under the scanner in other fields, too.

In July 2015, at the convocation ceremony of the Indian Institute of Science (IISc), NR Narayana Murthy, the co-founder of Infosys—a thirty-five-year-old IT company that has a market cap of around $34 billion[11] and employs more than 2,00,000 people[12]—ominously declared:

> ...let us pause and ask what the contributions of Indian institutions of higher learning, particularly IISc and IITs, have been over the last sixty plus years to make our society and the world a better place? Is there one invention from India that has become a hous old name in the globe? Is there one technology that has transformed the productivity of global corporations? Is there one idea that has led to an earth-shaking invention to delight global citizens? Folks, *the reality is that there is no such contribution from India in the last sixty years* [emphasis added].[13]

The observations of Narayana Murthy force us to question our two-faced education system and look for alternatives. Clearly, the hidden tunnel strategy, where millions of students give up on every little pleasure of life, is certainly not helping to produce the kind of specialists we need even in our present times. Hence, how we would tackle the challenging future with present learning approaches should be the topmost question in everyone's to-do list.

The Sad Story Of A Brilliant Mind

The story which I am going to narrate to you now is not from the world of fiction, but is a slice of the harsh and bitter reality resulting from walking alone in that dark tunnel—where there is hardly any option of giving up and where one walks with the enormous weight of expectation to always emerge as a winner. It is also a reflection of the monstrosity of our modern workplaces, which often treat human beings as mere cogs of a never resting, money-churning giant wheel.

Our story starts on 19 May 1992, with the birth of a lovable boy in a well-to-do family in one of the upscale residential colonies of South Delhi.

In India, parents are not only willing to realign their entire lives to ensure a successful trajectory for their children, but, many a time, they often want their own unfulfilled dreams and desires to be realised through their progeny. This is primarily because, with all the hardships they have gone through in their own lives, they want to ensure that their children do not bear the same—hence, the success of their children at each stage of life becomes paramount.

Ironically, sometimes parents' expectations create pressure on the very children they care for the most. Many a time, this expectation is not overt—not vocal—but even the simmering desires hidden deep inside the parents' hearts is enough to burden a child.

Perhaps the same happened in the case of this lovable boy.

The boy was endearingly named Sarvshreshth, a Sanskrit word that means 'the best among the best'.

Like other Indian parents, Sarvshreshth Gupta's parents, too, wanted the very best for him, and hence he had the opportunity to study in one of the leading public schools of India.

Sarvshreshth was excellent in school. He not only outperformed everyone in academics, but also in several extracurricular activities.

His brilliance did not go unnoticed, and he secured admission to an undergraduate course at the prestigious Wharton School of Business, USA—one of the best business schools in the world. For his father, 'it was a dream come true' as he 'had always wished and dreamed that one day' his son 'would study at an Ivy League college'.

At Wharton, Sarvshreshth tried his level best to cope with the gruelling schedule. In the four years he was at Wharton, he visited India only three times. Even the summers were dedicated to completing assignments. After all, in his father's words, he was on a 'mission, a task, an assignment. He was there to make his father proud'.

Sarvshreshth Gupta's determination helped him sail through Wharton, and he was now ready to bear the fruits of his hard work.

'Both of you go and take a dip in the holy Ganges. You have spent a lot on me in Indian currency, now I will earn in American dollars and return it all to you,' he had said to his parents during his final days at Wharton.

In 2014, at the young age of twenty-two, Sarvshreshth Gupta was snapped up—at a hefty package of upwards of US$ 100,000 (approximately 68 lac Indian rupees by the current conversion rate)—by Goldman Sachs, the sought-after financial firm where many young bright sparks dream of working.

However, Sarvshreshth Gupta's life at Goldman Sachs did not turn out to be as rosy as one would imagine.

With no scope for breaks, it was a life of sheer labour at the San Francisco office.

'Papa, I do not get enough sleep. I work twenty hours at a stretch,' he once communicated to his father, who obviously expressed his concern. But then, Sarvshreshth was there to prove he was not a weak mind. 'Come on Papa, I am young and strong. Investment banking is hard work,' he replied, determined to keep performing as he had always done in his life.

However, the burden of work started affecting even the sincerely dedicated Sarvshreshth Gupta. A few months into his job, he started complaining to his parents, 'This job is not for me. Too much work and too little time. I want to come back home.' His father was sympathetic, but perhaps feared that his son's desire to give up so soon would be seen as a reflection of his failure. 'Sonny, all are your age, young and ambitious, keep going,' he tried to counsel his son.

Around the third we of March 2015, Sarvshreshth Gupta couldn't take it anymore and submitted his resignation. His father was surprised, as he had not given Sarvshreshth 'an open mandate to quit'. Yet he tried to reassure his son, 'Sonny, I did not want you to quit, but now, since you have done so, we are with you. Come back home.'

But the father was still keen to know about his son's next steps and thus inquired, 'What do you want to do now?'

'I will rejuvenate myself, eat home-cooked food, walk and go to gym, and finally work with and expand our school,' the son replied.

The reply did not make his father too happy, as he did not want his son to quit and do non-serious activities at 'this stage of his career'. He desired his son to at least 'complete his one year at Goldman Sachs and learn something about corporate life'.

But then, this was not what he overtly said to his son.

'By a quirk of fate' Sarvshreshth Gupta was asked to reconsider his resignation, to which he agreed.

But sadly, nothing changed at Goldman Sachs.

During the late hours of the night of 16 April 2015, Sarvshreshth called his father again and expressed his agony, 'It is too much. I have not slept for two days, have a client meeting tomorrow morning, have to complete a presentation, my VP is annoyed and I am working alone in my office.'

His father was deeply annoyed with the trauma of his son and finally strongly asked Sarvshreshth to resign and come back home.

However, the resignation was never to come.

On 17 April, 2015, before the sun could rise, Sarvshreshth Gupta, who was yet to turn twenty-three, ended his life.[1]

***

The above sad account of brilliant Sarvshreshth Gupta is not mine but knitted on his father's open letter titled 'A Son Never Dies'[2] published a month after the sad demise of his son. Mr Gupta's self-reflective account serves as a caution to other parents on the dangers of the expectations today's generation must carry on their shoulders.[3]

The heartbreaking story reveals that there is no room for failure in our current approach to creating specialists. It also, in a way, shows how our brilliant minds are expected to walk on a set path and are judged no matter how uninspiring the journey is. Whereas, the lives of those mentioned in this book teach us that each learner has every right to explore, wander, withdraw or even fail at any juncture of their journey.

The tragic story of Sarvshreshth Gupta also forces us to question the eventual purpose of education and the yardstick by which we measure the success and failure of an educated person.

Should monetary translation be the only measurement of success or failure of a learner?

It seems that the only question one is interested in asking is about the kind of placement package available at the end of the degree. And so the colleges answer back in the same tone by advertising the salary a graduate can get at the end of a course as the only yardstick of their quality.

Even our top institutes are guilty of competing among each other only on the heftiness of the salaries of their graduates, and not on their ability to create innovative products, conduct pioneering research, invent life-saving drugs or provide creative solutions to the problems plaguing India.

How much room is there in our current education system for people wanting to try new things, spend their lives in search of answers to unanswered questions, create start-ups without fear of failure or train to be like our Metro Man, who chose to create world-class infrastructure for India and was happy working on an average government salary, when he could have easily beaten any of the students graduating with offers of topmost salaries?

In November 2017, Delhi's air quality deteriorated to carcinogenic levels. The pollution levels were ten times worse than those of Beijing—a city ill-famed for its pollution levels.[4] The Delhi Government termed the city a 'gas chamber'[5] and called for emergency measures. The irony is that Delhi had witnessed the same level of poor quality in the November of 2016 and several

Novembers of years before.[6] And the city had been called a 'gas chamber' in the previous years, too.[7]

Even with more than 2.5 million people dying every year due to pollution in India—the highest in the world[8]—we do not have very many specialists interested in providing a solution to this problem.

As the following example reflects, the weight of money-centric attitudes towards education must never be underestimated:

In March 2017, during a police investigation in a small village named Sangli, situated near the border of the states of Maharashtra and Karnataka, nineteen female foetuses were discovered buried next to a private hospital.[9] The investigation found that these were the result of female foeticide, committed by the doctor who owned the private hospital. These beautiful, innocent souls met this brutal fate because their parents did not want a girl child, and were assisted in this heinous crime sadly by a specialist.

As a coincidence, in September of the same year, in a report published by HSBC Bank, India was poised to become the third-largest economy in the world in 2028, surpassing Japan and Germany.[10]

And as we were rejoicing in our growth story, we failed to notice that, in the same year, on the Global Hunger Index (GHI), India ranked in the bottom twenty countries of the world, with more than 200 million (20 crore) hungry people.[11] In Asia, India's rank was only higher than Afghanistan and Pakistan.

Why, with such a strong growth rate and so many specialists, does India have one of the worst sex ratios in the world, and more than 15 per cent of its population has been going to bed hungry every day over the past several decades?

The
Fluid
Specialists

'Be Water, My Friend'
From smart city specialists to future cardiologists

Vishnudharmottaram Puranam is one of the lesser-known ancient Indian texts. Although the actual date of compilation is not known (with historians oscillating its period of origin between 1000 BC and 200 AD), the earliest written version is still considered to be, at least, around 2200 years old.

It may be quite right to assume that the long title may scare present-day readers, who may avoid the book, fearing it to be dense and boring. However, its text is written in almost a story form and is quite a simple and interesting read.

Even the long title is quite easy to understand.

In order to understand what the long Sanskrit title stands for, we can break it into four parts:

- *Vishnu* is simply the name of the Hindu God, to whom the text is dedicated.
- *Dharm* stands for what is considered to be righteous (not to

be confused with the current mistaken interpretation that it stands for religion).

- *Uttaram* stands for 'answer'.
- *Puranam* is often used as the suffix for ancient Indian texts, its interpreted translation being 'ancient or oldest form of literature'.

Thus the title *Vishnudharmottaram Puranam* simply means: an ancient text offered in the name of Vishnu that provides answers to what is righteous. However, it won't be wrong to term it as an encyclopedia on arts, sciences, architecture and philosophy. I request you all to refer to the back notes where I go into greater detail on the facts surrounding the *Puranam*.[1]

I request you keep the title in mind, as we will go into greater detail of the *Puranam* in the final chapters.

In most of the *purana*s, knowledge is transferred to the readers through lengthy conversations between sages and kings, where the questions follow answers and counter-questions. Interestingly, this method is starkly similar to that popularised by the ancient Gre scholars, particularly Socrates.[2]

In *Vishnudharmottaram Puranam*, which contains three parts and around 17,000 *shlokas*,[3] a similar method of transferring knowledge is followed.

One of the conversations in the *Puranam* is particularly interesting in the context of fluid specialisation.

Part 3 of the *Puranam*, which is called *Chitra Sutra*[4], contains a conversation between a sage called Rishi Markandeya and a king named Vajra.

Vajra, which literally means 'thunderbolt', was the great-grandson of Krishna. As per the ancient texts, after the epic battle of Mahabharata ended, as a result of a curse, the entire clan of Krishna perishes. Vajra remains the only surviving member.

At the same time, Dwarka, the capital city of Krishna's

kingdom, which was situated at the far west banks of the Arabian Sea, submerges into the oceanic waters.

Arjuna, the great warrior of the epic battle, takes Vajra to northern India, where he eventually establishes his kingdom—precisely in and around the area where the present holy city of Mathura is situated.

Although King Vajra enjoyed prosperity, he often experienced lengthy bouts of melancholy.

It was suggested to him that he establish imprints of Krishna all around Mathura to overcome the gloom. King Vajra then called for a learned sage, Rishi Markandeya, to explain to him the science and art of temple and statue building.

In *Chitra Sutra* (part 3 of *Vishnudharmottaram Puranam*), chapter 2, *shloka* 1–9, King Vajra presents his dilemma to Rishi Markandeya. The conversation flows to the following effect:

> King Vajra—'Oh! Sinless sage! Teach me the principles of statue building (*pratima lakshanam*) so that I can build a statue that is closest to the actual form of God.'

> Rishi Markandeya—'Oh! Great King! One who doesn't know the rules of sketching (*chitra*) cannot learn the principles of statue building.'

> King Vajra—'Then, first teach me the tenets of sketching.'

> Rishi Markandeya—'Oh! Successor of Lord Krishna! Without knowing the art of dancing (*nritya*), one cannot master the complexities of sketching (*chitra*).'

> King Vajra—'Then, first spill the knowledge on dancing (*nritya*).'

> Rishi Markandeya—'But then, one cannot understand the world of dancing (*nritya*) unless one masters the principles of musical instruments (*atodya*).'

> King Vajra—'Then, let me first learn about musical instruments (*atodya*) before moving on to dancing (*nritya*), sketching (*chitra*) and statue building (*pratima lakshanam*).'

Rishi Markandeya—'But then, unless the principles of singing (*geeta*) and the grammar of prose and verse (*gadya* and *padya*) are learned, one cannot proceed to learning about musical instruments.'

The circulatory nature of Rishi Markandeya's responses subtly points out that unless the integrative nature of all the disciplines and, in turn, the integrative nature of the universe is appreciated, one cannot master even a single discipline.

This is exactly the spirit of fluid specialisation.

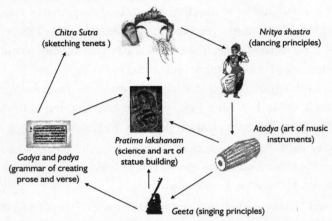

The interdisciplinary approach taught by Rishi Markandeya in *Chitra Sutra, Vishnudharmottaram Puranam,* chapter 2, shloka 1-9

***

The conversation excerpted from *Vishnudharmottaram* in favour of fluid approach may attract the criticism that, by being open to gathering from all disciplines, learners risk becoming jacks of all trades whereas, the current essence of education is to prepare nothing but specialists.

Interestingly, the phrase jack of all trades was first used, in 1592, for none other than William Shakespeare, by his contemporary writer named Robert Greene,[5] for his attempts to write in spite of lacking a degree and being a 'peasant'.[6] Shakespeare, who then worked as a newcomer actor and was attempting to establish himself as a playwright, was termed 'an upstart crow' in the same paragraph.

'Jack of all trades', because of its associative usage with the phrase 'master of none', has now taken on a negative connotation, more so in the case when one is expected to acquire advanced learning.

Teachers frequently warn their students that failure to rise higher on the degree ladder will eventually turn them into the 'jacks' of their respective careers. The current landscape of education almost works on this notion.

Being fluid does not mean being a jack. But then it surely demands not remaining unconcerned with other fields.

How do we strike this balance?

In one of his interviews, the belief-defying legendary martial artist superstar Bruce Lee expresses the advantage of being like water:

> 'Be formless, shapeless, like water. Now, you put water into a cup, it becomes the cup. You put water into a bottle it becomes the bottle. You put it in a teapot it becomes the teapot. Now, the water can flow or it can crash. Be water, my friend.'—Bruce Lee, 'The Lost Interview', 1971

Taking inspiration from the man who mastered his body as no one else did, I conceptualise fluid specialists—the kind of specialists we need to be—who are fluid enough to absorb from any subject but at the same time are as strong as water's crashing power in their expert area.

***

In the past few decades, a good number of scholarly minds have been working to resolve the conflict between generalists (jacks-of-all-trades who have a superficial understanding of many subjects) and specialists (who have a deep understanding of one subject).

In this process, a few models have been proposed for the benefit of a learner.

One such interesting model is the T-shaped approach to specialisation.[7]

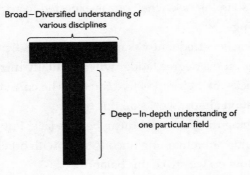

T-shaped model of specialisation (David Guest, 1991)

The T-shaped model simply expects that an individual should keep on acquiring in-depth knowledge in one particular discipline—represented by the long arm of the 'T'—and also at the same time be open enough to keep gathering from various fields—as reflected by the shorter arm of the 'T'.

While writing this chapter, I was doing my regular long walks, pondering the 'T' model of specialisation.

Although the 'T' model is certainly a step ahead of the one-dimensional specialist approach, I was not fully convinced by it. Yet I couldn't put my finger on exactly how it could be improved.

One day, while walking, I spotted a T-shaped piece of thin branch. I wasted no time in picking it up and bringing it back to my study.

I have a habit of collecting all sorts of things that eventually land in my study, because of which it has taken on the look of a magical, Harry-Potter-ish world, mashed with the flavour of Indian culture.

A few years ago, I noticed a beautiful antique spinning wheel—a *charkha*, as we call them in India.

Not many know that the spinning wheel, the earliest version of a machine, which can transform cotton fruits into threads and eventually into clothes, is an Indian invention.

A symbol of the inventive Indian mind, the antique *charkha* soon found a place in my study.

I was holding the T-shaped twig in my study when my eyes paused at the *charkha*. Suddenly, Bruce Lee's interpretation of the duality of water came to my mind. Not only did the shortcoming of the T-shaped model become clear to me, but the wheel symbolically metamorphosed into an improved specialisation model.

I term this model fluid-wheel.

Each of us specialists should draw our own fluid-wheel.

As illustrated below, the central hub of the fluid-wheel can be imagined as an individual's core specialisation area, whereas the spokes can represent all the various disciplines from which an individual can draw.

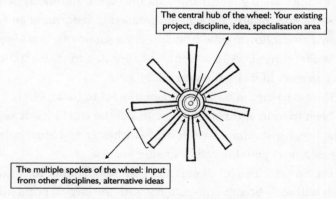

The central hub of the wheel: Your existing project, discipline, idea, specialisation area

The multiple spokes of the wheel: Input from other disciplines, alternative ideas

Fluid-wheel model of specialisation

The fluid-wheel tells me that obtaining specialisation is no different from how a spinning wheel converts fibre into yarn.

True specialisation is metaphorically equivalent to the beautiful process of spinning yarn from multiple fibres plucked from hundreds of cotton trees. The integrative nature of the final learning of a specialist is exactly like the woven yarn, which encompasses all material into it.

Crucially, while the T-shaped approach only suggests expanding knowledge, without any apparent connection to the specialised area, the fluid-wheel argues that all the diversified knowledge be brought towards the core specialisation area—the hub of the fluid-wheel (shown by inward-pointing arrows).

It is also a good time to clarify that fluidity doesn't mean that a child is enrolled into as many after-school classes as possible: I personally feel that such thoughtless enrolment puts too much stress on children and takes away their love of learning.

In order to test the practicability of the fluid-wheel, let's try applying it to a very popular futuristic idea—the building of smart cities, which is currently under large-scale implementation in India.

***

In 2015, the Indian government announced the ambitious Smart Cities Mission. Briefly, the scheme entailed transforming an area within a city, following the principles of a smart city. A budget of INR 98,000 crore (US$ 14 billion) was allocated to create 100 such smart areas in India by the year 2022.[8]

The smart-city initiatives are not limited to India, but have also been tried in various leading cities of the world (such as Singapore, Amsterdam, Barcelona, Manchester and Stockholm, to name a few) with limited or greater success.

The Smart Cities Mission is a golden opportunity for India, which will soon become the country with the largest population in the world, to create a futuristic model of urban habitation, which can then be replicated to build an India with a vision of several centuries.

Thus, a crucial question to ask is—

Do we have or are we preparing smart-city specialists who can deliver a vision for India that can last for centuries?

And before an answer is attempted another question to be asked is—

Who exactly can be termed a smart-city specialist?

Are these architects? Urban planners? Engineers? IT specialists? Builders? Bureaucrats? Entrepreneurs? Environmentalists?

How about including a sociologist in the list, as well? Yes, sociologist.

Those who are not from the field of urban planning may not know that the first master plans of almost eighteen Indian cities[9] (including the city of Indore)[10] were conceived not by an architect, but by a college drop-out sociologist named Peter Geddes.

Born in the year 1854 in Scotland, Geddes never took a formal degree in sociology but studied animal sciences under TH Huxley, Charles Darwin's friend, the same man under whom HG Wells was trained as well.

Geddes taught himself sociology, which he then brought into the field of urban planning. The combination helped Geddes to become one of the 'founding fathers of the British town planning movement'.[11]

Interestingly, Geddes drew inspiration from the ancient Indian philosophy of holism[12] (as also reflected in the conversation between Rishi Markandeya and King Vajra in *Vishnudharmottaram Puranam*) and argued that a plan of a city cannot be conceived unless market economics, the social and cultural aspects of human society and other key elements of our existence are interplayed with the principles of town planning.

For Geddes (1917), a city was like a flower—'inseparable and interwoven'—and he criticised the isolated approach of specialists who wanted to isolate this flower into various petals:

Each of the various specialists remains too closely concentrated upon his single specialism, too little awake to those of the others. Each sees clearly and seizes firmly upon one petal of the six-lobed flower of life and tears it apart from the whole.[13]

Geddes considered 'healthy and happy' families to be the eventual aim of an urban planner and brought the social consequences of urbanisation and industrialisation (such as crime, redundancy, and weakened nuclear family and social fabric) to the centre of urban planning.

Geddes' work confirms that our smart-city specialists need to be truly fluid specialists, bringing possible forces into consideration and keeping the 'happy and healthy' citizen at the core of the fluid-wheel.

Thus, a fluid smart-city specialist would consider principles of market forces, citizen well-being, non-discrimination, sustainable development, good governance, inclusion, equality, urban planning, affordable education, happy workplaces, stress-free commutes, artificial intelligence, renewable energy, etc. He or she would not blindly decide to create monotonous skyscrapers, but would be open to including the sociocultural flavour of all Indian traditions.

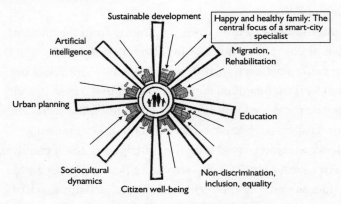

The fluid-wheel of a smart-city specialist

We can even create an imaginary scene in which King Vajra is interested in building a smart city and requests that Rishi Markandeya explain to him the principles of building such a place. Rishi Markandeya, in the true fluid spirit, would have replied:

> Before putting the brick, concrete and iron together, you must first learn about sustainable development. However, as soon as you decide to explore the harmony of the relationship between humans and nature, you would realise that you must train yourself in the tenets of good governance. But, as soon as you would prepare yourself to learn good governance, you would realise that it is crucial for you to first educate yourself in the principles of non-discrimination, inclusion and equality.

The strength of a model is its universal applicability. The more I thought about and perfected the fluid-wheel, the more I was convinced of its utility to specialists from almost all the fields—when a writer is building a story (as how HG Wells did), a director is thinking about a film project (technical, commercial, artistic aspects), an architect is conceptualising a building project (similar to a smart-city expert), a company is making an innovative product, a state is making a policy, a person or an organisation is building a strategy, etc.

To elaborate, let us see how the model may be useful for doctors in the changing future. We can pick the field of cardiology—the branch of medicine that deals with the heart and associated circulatory system.

For a cardiologist, as shown in the illustration below, the hub of the fluid-wheel could be the human heart, and the spokes could denote all those areas from which he can learn to keep a heart going on forever. The spokes could be what the knowledge he or she draws from all possible disciplines, without any bias.

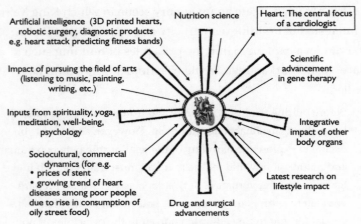

Artificial intelligence (3D printed hearts, robotic surgery, diagnostic products e.g. heart attack predicting fitness bands)

Nutrition science

Heart: The central focus of a cardiologist

Impact of pursuing the field of arts (listening to music, painting, writing, etc.)

Scientific advancement in gene therapy

Inputs from spirituality, yoga, meditation, well-being, psychology

Integrative impact of other body organs

Sociocultural, commercial dynamics (for e.g.
• prices of stent
• growing trend of heart diseases among poor people due to rise in consumption of oily street food)

Latest research on lifestyle impact

Drug and surgical advancements

The fluid-wheel of a cardiologist

As shown in the illustration above, to start with, a fluid cardiologist does not restrict himself to conducting heart surgeries (as we saw in the case of Yogini's father, Dr Roy) but keeps himself at the forefront of research—keeping himself abreast of inter-branch, inter-field advancements, even within the wider domain of medicine.[14] He is also well aware of interdisciplinary advancements in fields such as genetics[15] and epigenetics,[16] and their applicability in cardiology.

Importantly, such a cardiologist is open-minded to understand the implications of fields that may not be directly linked to biology, such as artificial intelligence and 3D printing. Hence, he is quite aware of the advent of 3D-printed hearts or personalised diagnostic instruments such as fitness bands with the ability to pre-alert the user to potential heart attacks, etc.

He is also not dogmatic towards alternative medicine and may be open to drawing from areas such as yoga, spirituality and meditation.

Finally, such a cardiologist is also well aware of sociocultural and commercial dynamics influencing the world of heart diseases.

For example, he understands the dynamics of why heart-saving drugs, surgeries and devices (such as pacemakers, stents, etc.) are expensive and out of the reach of many poor people.[17]

As days passed by, I kept devising fluid-wheels for other fields too. The exercise was helpful because it took me to the doors of a school situated in New York—a school which has a unique record as far as the world of specialists goes.

The School That Produces The Highest Number Of Nobel Laureates

The Bronx High School of Science, situated in New York, USA, has the distinction of producing the highest number of Nobel Prize winners in the world. In its eighty-year existence, the Bronx School has produced a total of eight Nobel Prize winners, including seven in Physics and one in Chemistry. Just to put things in perspective, India, to date, has only five Nobel Prize winners:[1]

1. Rabindranath Tagore (in Literature)
2. CV Raman (in Physics)
3. Mother Teresa (in Peace)
4. Amartya Sen (in Economics)
5. Kailash Satyarthi (in Peace)

A Nobel Prize is usually awarded to those extraordinary individuals and organisations that have extended the frontiers of human excellence and understanding. It can be considered the ultimate badge of approval for a specialist.

With seven Nobel Prizes in Physics, it might be assumed that students at the Bronx School are only focused on studying physics. And as per the hidden-tunnel strategy followed by many specialisation-se ers, the students at Bronx must only be studying other subjects just to pass exams. They would surely not be participating in any extracurricular activities and would have no interaction with the social sciences whatsoever.

However, a close analysis of the Bronx School's curriculum proves all these specialist-making myths to be absolutely incorrect.

In usual schools, students start leaning towards their choice of subject cohort even long before Year 10, when the separation actually takes place. Once the barrier of tenth standard is crossed, the chances of interacting with subjects from the other cohorts become absolutely negligible.

No such separation takes place at the Bronx School.

The students at Bronx not only study pure sciences but are also required to take compulsory courses in the social sciences, foreign languages and fine arts. In addition, the school offers a staggering range of more than 160 distinct courses as electives to its students.

Unlike our boring, flavourless, stress-inducing coaching factories, Bronx is throbbing with extracurricular activities. The Bronx School has approximately 100 student clubs covering sports, music, arts and awareness. It boasts more than ten sports clubs ranging from chess to badminton, seven music and arts-related clubs, and eleven youth awareness clubs that introduce students to key challenges faced by humanity on the global level. The school also publishes more than four journals of various types, along with student magazines.

Those students who are keen to participate in school debates must not give up on their passion. They must take a cue from students at Bronx, who have performed exceptionally well, winning several awards, including many national competitions.

The students who plunge themselves into the dark alleys of the hidden track by giving up on extracurricular activities and stripping themselves of any scope for living in a magical, cozy bubble might be surprised to learn that the school with the most Nobel laureates also has an active student club dedicated to Harry Potter.

If we move away from the Bronx example and try se ing specific examples of fluidity among other Nobel Prize winners, we stumble onto an increasing number of laureates who advocate drawing knowledge from other disciplines towards one's core area.

One such reflection appears in the words of Martin Chalfie, who was awarded the Nobel Prize in Chemistry in 2008,:

> The best training I received in college did not come only from my sciences courses, but from the social science and humanities courses I took.[2]

Chalfie, who calls himself a neurogeneticist, also highlights how he wants to travel beyond his narrow field and work with 'physicists and engineers':

> I am very interested in collaborating with physicists and engineers to investigate how the sensor works. Having good collaborators means that I don't need or even want to become an expert in every field that touches my work. I just need to be open and interested.[3]

William E Moerner, who won the 2014 Nobel Prize in Chemistry, was actually an electrical engineer who, in fact, spent more time in college studying physics and maths than chemistry. Moerner loves music and theatre and considers them an absolutely essential part of his life.

Like Chalfie, Moerner too considers the interrelatedness of subjects crucial for future scientists:

It is still critical to deeply focus on a particular area to become an expert...but at the same time, I believe that it is very powerful to learn other fields of science on the side.... Many of the most exciting discoveries are appearing at the interfaces between fields.[4]

Francis Crick, the Nobel laureate who co-discovered the double-helix structure of the DNA molecule, actually graduated in physics. He considered that his background in physics helped him decipher the DNA molecule with ease, while other biologists found the structures complex and difficult to compr end due to their lack of understanding of the fundamentals of physics.

The deeper I analysed the work of Nobel Prize-winners, the more I was convinced that our world needs fluid specialists.

And soon, I found one Nobel laureate who dazzled me with his remarkable ability to fetch pearls of wisdom from several diversified streams and draw them towards his core interest areas.

As Mahatma Gandhi would spin his charkha to inspire an entire nation to come together to fight for its independence, this wise man has intertwined threads of varied disciplines to weave outstanding benefits for mankind.

He is none other than the exceptional Amartya Sen, our next fluid specialist.

*****

Marie Curie (1867–1934), a Polish woman who was born into a family of teachers, was the first woman to win a Nobel Prize, the only woman to win it twice and the only person in history to win the prize in two different categories (Physics and Chemistry).

Marie worked with her husband, Pierre Curie, and they were both responsible for the discovery of radioactive elements—radium and polonium.[5]

It was Marie who coined the term 'radioactivity',[6] and the first application of a radioactive element in the treatment of cancer took place under her direction. The discovery led her and her husband to jointly receive the Nobel in 1903.

It is interesting to note that the Nobel committee had initially ignored Marie's name; it was only on the insistence of Swedish mathematician Magnus Goesta Mittag-Leffler, a champion of women's rights, and the written complaint of her husband that her name was rightly included.[7]

Marie was an active partner and supporter of her husband, who also worked in the field of sound. It was through Pierre's pioneering work on high-frequency sound waves, called 'ultrasound', that the field of medical diagnostics witnessed groundbreaking progress.[8] The non-invasive ultrasound machines, through which one can see inside a human body, use Pierre's research.

One such machine, (commonly known as the 'sonography' or 'ultrasound' in India) was invented with a totally innocent motive—to monitor a foetus in the womb to ensure its well-being.

But, in India, this innocent machine was used for an entirely opposite and most evil purpose.

Marie Curie is undoubtedly one of the brightest shining examples for women's rights and education. She would have never even dreamt that one day her husband's research would, ironically, form the basis of a machine that would be used to prevent a girl child from even coming into this world, let alone flourishing and creating a name for herself like Marie.

In 1990, a mere six-page essay exposed one of the most heinous secrets of India.[9] The essay revealed that the Indian population census is 'missing' around 3.7 crore (37 million) women.[10]

Apart from the fact that a girl child will often die as her nutrition and well-being are neglected on the basis that she is not a he, the key reason for the 'missing women' of India is the killing of girl children in the womb itself.

Sonography machines were being used by specialist doctors to diagnose the sex of unborn children who would then be aborted quickly if they happened to be girls.

This is exactly what the doctor from Sangli did.

The essay shook the country's very consciousness, and it wasted no time in passing a strict law against female foeticide. In the past twenty-five years or so, several NGOs and individuals have come forward to raise awareness against this evil practice.

Yet, tragically, the number of 'missing women' continued to grow. Today, this number is estimated to be around 50 million (5 crore). Just to put the number in perspective, this is more than the entire population of countries such as Canada, Spain, South Korea or Argentina.

The phenomenon of 'missing women' was brought to the world's notice not by a medical specialist but an economist—Amartya Sen—who has since not stopped championing the cause of women's rights.

Gender inequality is not the only area in which Amartya Sen contributes; his work has enhanced our understanding of justice, liberty, democracy, polity, education, people's well-being, parity, poverty, etc., permeating the very foundation on which our civilisation actually rests.

In order to understand what shapes Amartya Sen's profound thinking, I thought of an interesting and rather fun exercise.

I decided to get inside the mind of Amartya Sen!

My job would have been really easy if I had an ultrasound machine that could reveal the building blocks of his thought processes, but as we haven't yet invented such a machine, I thought of using an alternative method.

I simply went through Amartya Sen's writings and tried identifying those autobiographical elements that could help me understand how his mind works.

This exercise is only attempted to help my readers get closer to his mind and, one never knows, perhaps in the process it may inspire a few to follow his path and achieve the coveted prize.

***

Amartya, which means immortal in Sanskrit, was born in the year 1933 inside the womb of one of the most progressive learning centres of India of those times. According to Sen, this was the place where his 'educational attitudes were formed.'[11]

There was no place for a hidden tunnel in this groundbreaking educational campus, nor any room for those interested in a competitive exam mindset.

Here, one just needed to be 'curious' (Sen, 2014), and certainly not a rank holder.

The 'towering' founder of this educational campus with 'many sides', as Sen (2014) calls him, disliked the submergence of the Indian cultural ethos under the wave of the Western model of education. Hence, he wanted a school that could introduce the students to the cultural glory of India. However, the founder was not blinded by the pride he carried for India, but considered that the whole world has a lot to offer a child. He wanted his school to be:

> ...the connecting thread between India and the world...[truly] a world centre for the study of humanity somewhere beyond the limits of nation and geography.[12]

Sen felt fortunate to be a student in this path-breaking school that brought the right mix of West and East, and that taught him not to limit himself to one discipline, one view of the world, one dimension or one identity, but to explore as widely as possible.

The place was rightly called Visva Bharati, which means the unity of the world and India. Its founder was none other than the poet, philosopher, writer, painter and first Nobel laureate of India, the educational reformist Rabindranath Tagore.

Tagore established Visva Bharati in Shantiniketan, a small town situated in present West Bengal, on a tract of land that was bought by his father for 1 Indian rupee in 1862 to establish a spiritual ashram.[13]

Rabindranath Tagore, who gave the title of Mahatma to revered Gandhi, is the only person in the world who is credited with penning the national anthem of two countries, namely India and Bangladesh, and co-writing that of a third, Sri Lanka.

Tagore, in a way, the guru of Amartya Sen, was truly fluid.

Tagore spent his formative years reading varied subjects from anatomy to mathematics to Sanskrit, but hated formal education.

He spent just one day in college and instead wandered for months, covering the length and breadth of India.

And when his father sent him to the UK to become a barrister, instead of spending his time in college, he submerged himself in the writings of Shakespeare and other English writers, only to come back to India degreeless.

In spite of being a philosopher-writer, Tagore leaned towards sciences. He spent the later years of his life learning the basic tenets of physics, chemistry and biology—several of his stories and poems twined around scientific themes.

Always keen to experiment with new fields, Tagore picked up painting seriously at the age of forty but found himself wanting. He mentions his keenness to try this new field in one of his letters to the famous scientist and his friend JC Bose:

> But, just as a mother lavishes most affection on her ugliest son, so I feel secretly drawn to the very skill that comes to me least easily.[14]

Unsuccessful in his endeavour, Tagore gave up painting only to pick it up again at the ripe age of sixty and eventually created several masterpieces.

In fact it was Tagore who not only named Amartya but also taught him to be curious, exploratory and not to tie himself with the ropes of one particular identity.

Tagore disliked trapping a child inside a concrete classroom as, for him, a human mind inside four walls was far away from the beauty of nature. Hence, taking inspiration from ancient Indian *gurukul*s, he created a learning place amidst dense trees, comprising of dusty trails on which his students could walk for hours and contemplate the true purpose of education.

Amartya Sen's strong support for gender equality was shaped in Tagore's Visva Bharati, which happened to be a co-ed school, and provided a 'cosmopolitan' (Sen, 2014) environment for women. Amartya Sen's mother, who had also been a student in Shantiniketan, learned judo, which in his words 'would have been very unusual in the 1920s'.[15] Similarly, his grandmother was an educated, independent woman who worked as an expert midwife.

Sen's maternal grandfather was a Sanskrit teacher at Visva Bharati, thanks to whom he mastered the language and could read ancient Indian texts with dexterity right from an early age. Soon, he was in love with the richness of Indian arts and culture. He noticed the scholarly nature of the arguments inside the ancient Indian texts, with multiple points of view and conflicting ideas existing peacefully together. The fact that Vedic literature not only provided answers but also contained several unanswered inquiries shaped his rational and accommodating thinking.

His command over Sanskrit also introduced him to the vastly advanced ancient Indian mathematics, which he fell in love with. He was amazed by the vast strides Indian mathematicians of early times had made ahead of their counterparts from other parts of the world. For instance, he notes that Varahamihira, a sixth-century mathematician, was both precise and very close to the right answer when he calculated that a year comprises 365.25875 days.[16]

After winning a Nobel, each recipient is asked to give something to the Nobel foundation museum on long-term loan. For Amartya Sen, one item was his school bicycle, on which he rode under the shadow of the dense trees of Shantiniketan, roaming aimlessly, contemplating his reading material and life. The second item was a book containing pioneering work on mathematics by eminent Indian mathematician Aryabhata, which Sen considers 'one of the great Sanskrit classics on mathematics from 499 AD'.[17] One can notice an echo of the fluid approach in Sen's following recollection of his childhood memories:

> …in my school days I was deeply involved with the study of Sanskrit, on one side, and with mathematical and analytical reasoning, on the other.[18]

> …I was enchanted by Sanskrit literature (mostly classical Sanskrit). Reading Panini was as exciting an adventure as any I have undertaken in my life—it taught me the basic demands of intellectual discipline.[19]

Thanks to the multicultural and stress-free environment of Tagore's Visva Bharati, there was no pressure on young Sen to become a specialist and choose his subjects accordingly. So he immersed himself in the writings of Buddha and was 'bowled over by the clarity of reasoning'.[20]

One can only wonder how many children in our current schools who aim to become economists would be allowed to read Buddha and include this perspective in their fluid-wheel of economics?

But Sen did not face any such restrictions; he was free to choose his books and read, not to pass an exam, because there weren't any in his school. Hence, he did not fear books but treated them almost like toys. While a child in school today dreads reading mathematics, Sen recollects the name of Euclid, the famous ancient Gre mathematician, with utter fondness.

And as, perhaps, a child today would do anything to visit the Warner Brother's Harry Potter studio in London, to be transported into a Harry Potter world, Amartya Sen felt the same when thinking of being transported back in time to ancient Greece, to the times when Euclid was alive:

> I would have given everything to get a ticket to ancient Greece to go and invade the privacy of Euclid.[21]

The freedom also allowed the future economist to read stories from all around the world. Right from reading almost everything that the English writer George Bernard Shaw wrote, Sen let the stories of Russian writer Leo Tolstoy introduce him to the concepts of social justice, parity and liberty, which he later brought towards his core area.

The way the young Amartya moved with ease between the worlds created by Kalidasa, Aryabhata, Euclid, Bernard Shaw, Leo Tolstoy and others truly explains how he could eventually create interconnectivity between diverse topics ranging from justice, freedom, parity and democracy to welfare and bring them all towards his core area of economics.

Sen was only nine years old when the dreadful Bengal famine occurred, killing more than 3 million (30 lac) people. His mind had probably already attained the sensitivity to notice that these were largely those people who were absolutely plunged at the bottom of poverty. Decades later, he returned to the data from those times and proved that so many people died not because there was not enough food, but because this food was not made available to them. His work became the basis for saving millions of lives around the world, with international agencies, governments and NGOs incorporating policies to mitigate lopsidedness in food distribution.

When Sen arrived at Cambridge to do his doctorate in economics, he reflected on the true power of his evolved learning under Tagore and did not subject himself to one camp or one economic ideology, but embraced them all:

I had chosen to apply to Trinity after noticing, in the handbook of Cambridge University, that three remarkable economists of very different political views coexisted there.[22]

He even 'took the radical decision of studying philosophy in that period' (Sen, 1998), which he found truly 'rewarding' (Sen, 1998) and profoundly useful in his work on economics.

Finally, the scan of Bharat Ratna Amartya Sen's brain is not complete without a mention of his fighting spirit. He was struck with cancer of the mouth at the young age of eighteen and again at thirty-seven, but emerged victorious on both occasions.

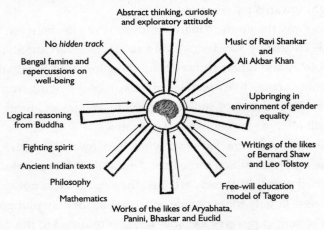

Amartya Sen's fluid-wheel: The elements which shaped his thinking

The lessons from the Bronx School and the lives of Rabindranath Tagore and Amartya Sen inspire us to rethink the path we currently take to become a specialist. One never knows, as we live the journey of trying, failing, rising, failing and trying again, we may become the kind of a specialist we never dreamt to be.

The Bigger
Fluid Questions

What Can We Learn From The Richest Man In The World And The Boy Who Broke The IIT-IIM Mould

India has always been a land of storytellers. For thousands of years, life lessons were taught to children through simple stories and fables, where no boundaries are drawn in terms of who is eventually giving the message—it could be anyone from a tree to an animal to a simple rock to the moon or even a God.

One such famous character, whose stories have travelled from generations to generations, is Tenali Rama.

Tenali Rama was actually a fifteenth-century Telugu poet and writer from the southwest region of India,[1] known for his witty personality. Several short stories based on the life experiences of Tenali Rama have taken the form of folklore.

One such story is from Tenali Rama's childhood, when he found himself in front of none other than Goddess Kali.

Tenali Rama was a ten-year-old boy when he was instructed

by a sage to visit a deserted temple and chant mantras, calling upon the goddess of power—Kali.

Tenali Rama followed the instructions and spent days without food or water, praying to Kali.

Pleased with Tenali Rama's devotion, the Goddess appeared in person to bless the boy.

Kali—with several heads and hands, burning red eyes and a necklace of human heads—bears quite a fearsome appearance.

However, instead of being scared, little Tenali started laughing. Seeing this, Kali was angered and demanded an answer from the boy. Tenali Rama asked for her forgiveness and explained that he couldn't control his laughter because he was thinking about how the Goddess, with her several heads, would wipe her noses if she caught a cold, when for him even to manage one nose was difficult.

The answer made Goddess Kali laugh. Happy with Tenali Rama's bold innocence, she presented him with two bowls—one filled with milk and the other with honey—and asked him to choose one.

'The honey bowl will bring immense wealth to you, whereas the milk bowl will make you the most knowledgeable person around,' said the Goddess to the little Tenali.

Being a clever boy, Tenali requested of the Goddess that he be allowed to taste the contents of both bowls before making his choice. Kali smiled, agreed and disappeared, but not before blessing Tenali Rama so that he would not only be the wisest but also the wealthiest.

The moral of the story, as conveyed to the children, is that wealth without wisdom would eventually bring misery to one's life, whereas one who enjoyed wisdom without the perks of wealth would always struggle to make his ends meet in this material world.

In the ancient Indian moral stories, wealth is always contrasted with knowledge.

It may confuse some that knowledge stands almost opposed to wealth.

For example, ancient Indian texts also include stories where the worshippers of Lakshmi—the Goddess of Wealth—and the worshippers of Saraswati—the Goddess of Knowledge—often find themselves pursuing opposite ends. That is, if knowledge is chased, prosperity starts slipping away, and if a person is too obsessed with acquiring wealth, he fails to pursue the path of knowledge.

In fact, if we think deeply, we will realise that the intent of the Tenali Rama story, and other such stories, is to point out to readers the contrast between personal gain and public good.

That is, whether we are learning or working, how often are we thinking of personal gain (wealth) and how often are we thinking of the public good (wisdom)?

In ancient Indian texts, the Sanskrit word for public good is *lok kalyanam* (*lok* means world and *kalyanam*, benefit).

A reader of these texts is often posed a value question—how many of our actions are for *lok kalyanam*?

This is exactly what the Metro Man is asking from those 6000-odd engineering colleges. What he meant, perhaps, was that the path of *lok kalyanam* is not pursued by the majority of colleges, which eventually results in the mediocrity of engineering education in India.

In fact, we all face this value question, whether we are working for others or for ourselves.

In my personal journey, like everyone else, I too struggle to resolve the contrast of making money for myself and *lok kalyanam*.

For example, when I am deeply submerged in the process of writing just one small paragraph, what is it that is driving me to write it? Should I write that paragraph with the intention of bringing material gain to myself, or should I write it with the aim of igniting millions of minds?

The message emerging from the story of Tenali Rama, of having the right mix of honey and milk in life, is truly a step ahead in resolving the conflict between wealth and the greater good.

It is true that a balance is needed. But, perhaps, the story falls a little short in telling us the exact proportion of the balance.

In order to resolve this deficiency, I tried to weave my own little moral lesson, which may be useful to strike the right balance of wealth and the greater good in the modern environment.

***

Following the traditions adopted by the ancient storytellers of India, I present to you two kinds of bulls. One is called the Money bull and the other is the Knowledge bull. But these are no ordinary bulls.

Both bulls have an extremely high appetite and remain hungry most of the time; hence, they constantly travel in search of food. However, each bull eats a different kind of food. The heads of the bulls are different from the rest of their bodies. And as the head also has the mouth, this is what determines their preferred food.

The Money bull is always in search of money. Before every action and every thought, the head of the Money bull asks, 'Will this generate money?'. Whether it is selecting a discipline, choosing a career, starting a company, shaping a project or inventing a product, it is money that drives and money that carves the path of the Money bull.

If fodder for the Money bull is absent, its desire to work evaporates. As the body of a bull is always b ind the head, for the Money bull *lok kalyanam* always comes after money.

On the other hand, the Knowledge bull is constantly in search of knowledge and its application to the greater good. Before every action and every thought, the head of the Knowledge bull asks, 'Will this contribute to the greater good?'. Whether it is selecting a discipline, choosing a career, starting a company, shaping a project or inventing a product, it is the greater good that drives and the greater good that decides.

For the Knowledge bull, *lok kalyanam* always comes before money.

In terms of learning, the Money bull travels in those directions where he can find maximum money, and only gathers knowledge (through the choice of a degree or course, for instance) that would help him to travel on the money path.

Whereas, the Knowledge bull travels in those directions where he can find maximum knowledge and only gathers money when that would help him to travel on the *lok kalyanam* path.

The more I thought about the great inventors and great artists the world has seen, and the examples of great minds from this book, the more strongly I felt that most of them worked as Knowledge bulls and not as Money bulls. Yes, many of them were immensely successful, rich and famous, but it all came because they were obsessed with furthering the frontiers of knowledge for the greater good.

For example, it was Charles Darwin's unquenched thirst to know and not his obsession with becoming rich that made him choose to unravel the mysteries of evolution. He could have easily inherited the established medical practice that had made his father extremely rich.

Not many would know that Rabindranath Tagore was born in a family that was among the richest in India. His grandfather was the first Indian to become a bank director, in a bank he himself owned. When Tagore was born, his family's massive landholding spanned three states. Incidentally, Rabindranath's grandfather was a ruthless *zamindar*[2]—a Money bull who never waived his land rent no matter how poor the farmers remained. Rabindranath Tagore inherited the same *zamindari*. However, unlike his grandfather, *zamindar* Rabindranath was a Knowledge bull. He understood the plight of the poor farmers and often collected only token rents from them. In fact, while he spent his time away from home and among his vast landholdings, he penned stories and poems depicting the atrocities of *zamindari* inflicted on poor farmers. Indeed, he chose to put the land to better use, an example of which can be seen in the form of Shantiniketan.

And if one were to analyse what kind of bull our Metro Man E Sreedharan is, one need only look at his simple life and measure it against the unfortunately high ranking held by India on the world index of corruption.[3] When E Sreedharan headed Konkan Railways, he decided to work for less than 10,000 rupees per month. As ironic as it may sound, the Indian government decided to make a monthly deduction of 4000 rupees from his salary.[4] The Metro Man had no option but to approach the courts, where his advocate pointed that after tax and other deductions, the monthly take-home salary of the most renowned infrastructure specialist of India was just 1080 rupees. It was only at the b est of the courts that he managed to get his token salary. Yet, this Knowledge bull decided to forget the bitter experience, and gave India the Delhi Metro.

In the previous chapter, we had built the fluid-wheel for a cardiologist. One of the spokes of that wheel, which a cardiologist should incorporate in his learning, is curbing the rise of unethical practices in the field.

In India, the practice of medicine, including the field of cardiology, suffers a severe lack of trust due to the malpractices of many doctors. There have been thousands of cases where patients have been advised to submit to unrequired, expensive diagnostic and surgical procedures. In fact, not only in India but even in the USA, it has been reported that 'millions of Americans...have undergone unnecessary elective surgery including pacemaker implants, coronary bypass surgery, hysterectomies and Caesarean section'.[5]

Recently, the Indian government capped the prices of stents[6] in order to prevent undue profit making by hospitals and stent-selling companies. Incidentally, this did not happen due to a cardiologist but through the efforts of a lawyer named Birender Sangwan.

In 2014, while visiting a friend who had recently had a stent installed, Sangwan was shocked to discover the hefty cost charged by the hospital—while the same stent was available for 23,000 INR, the hospital had charged 1,26,000 INR for it.[7] This led Sangwan to file a public interest litigation (PIL). It was this PIL that eventually steered the government to put a ceiling on the prices of stents.[8]

Truly, India needs more Knowledge bulls like our Metro Man E Sreedharan and lawyer Birender Sangwan.

In order to further test the strength of the Knowledge bull approach, I decided to apply it to the richest man in the world. The exercise revealed some interesting results, which may be useful for all of us.

***

On 3 February 1976, an open letter published by Bill Gates, a young twenty-one-year-old software specialist who had recently founded Microsoft, clearly revealed how strong his ambition to earn money was.

Gates had been successful in developing a computer interpreter. For those, like me, who do not have a clue what this means, an interpreter[9] can be understood by comparing it to a basic capability of the human brain. For example, once a human brain learns how to calculate 2 + 2 = 4 and 3 + 3 = 6, it retains the arithmetic principles in its memory, and if next time it is asked what 2 + 3 is, it can generate the answer on the basis of those retained principles. An interpreter provides a similar kind of capability to a computer (i.e., on the machine level itself), such that if a computer is asked the same question, it already has the arithmetic principles, which were written in the form of an interpreter (so that it need not be written every time a new software is created).

Gates was one of the first people in the world to develop an interpreter for small-sized microcomputers (compared to the sizes we see today, the computers before the 1970s were giant). The reduction in the size of a computer created the tremendous opportunity for them to become a hous old item. And as an interpreter was almost like a mini-brain for a microcomputer, it could easily be sold to all those wanting to manufacture such computers.

Although Gates had started selling his interpreter in the thousands, for almost US$ 150 (1000 Indian rupees in 1975) per software license, he was not at all happy that a large number of people were using it for free.

These people were largely hobbyists, who were assembling computers as freelancers. These were early days of small computers and the rules of the game were still being laid.

Gates responded with a bitter open letter detailing how the hours he and his team had spent coding the interpreter translated into a staggering cost of US$ 40,000 (around 3 lac Indian rupees in 1976), and that free usage is as good as stealing. The young Gates made no effort to hide his anger:

As the majority of hobbyists must be aware, most of you steal your software.[10]

The open letter was widely circulated and generated mixed reactions.

The hobbyists argued that if the interpreter weren't available for free, they wouldn't have used it in the first place, and in turn gave the logic that Gates' interpreter was only popular because it was being widely used by hobbyists.

-2-

February 3, 1976

An Open Letter to Hobbyists

To me, the most critical thing in the hobby market right now is the lack of good software courses, books and software itself. Without good software and an owner who understands programming, a hobby computer is wasted. Will quality software be written for the hobby market?

Almost a year ago, Paul Allen and myself, expecting the hobby market to expand, hired Monte Davidoff and developed Altair BASIC. Though the initial work took only two months, the three of us have spent most of the last year documenting, improving and adding features to BASIC. Now we have 4K, 8K, EXTENDED, ROM and DISK BASIC. The value of the computer time we have used exceeds $40,000.

The feedback we have gotten from the hundreds of people who say they are using BASIC has all been positive. Two surprising things are apparent, however. 1) Most of these "users" never bought BASIC (less than 10% of all Altair owners have bought BASIC), and 2) The amount of royalties we have received from sales to hobbyists makes the time spent of Altair BASIC worth less than $2 an hour.

Why is this? As the majority of hobbyists must be aware, most of you steal your software. Hardware must be paid for, but software is something to share. Who cares if the people who worked on it get paid?

Is this fair? One thing you don't do by stealing software is get back at MITS for some problem you may have had. MITS doesn't make money selling software. The royalty paid to us, the manual, the tape and the overhead make it a break-even operation. One thing you do do is prevent good software from being written. Who can afford to do professional work for nothing? What hobbyist can put 3-man years into programming, finding all bugs, documenting his product and distribute for free? The fact is, no one besides us has invested a lot of money in hobby software. We have written 6800 BASIC, and are writing 8080 APL and 6800 APL, but there is very little incentive to make this software available to hobbyists. Most directly, the thing you do is theft.

What about the guys who re-sell Altair BASIC, aren't they making money on hobby software? Yes, but those who have been reported to us may lose in the end. They are the ones who give hobbyists a bad name, and should be kicked out of any club meeting they show up at.

I would appreciate letters from any one who wants to pay up, or has a suggestion or comment. Just write me at 1180 Alvarado SE, #114, Albuquerque, New Mexico, 87108. Nothing would please me more than being able to hire ten programmers and deluge the hobby market with good software.

Bill Gates

Bill Gates
General Partner, Micro-Soft

Open letter published by Bill Gates

The entire controversy was also well exploited by Steve Jobs, the founder of Apple computers. An ad was immediately published in newspapers, highlighting that his company's computers came with free interpreters.

Apple Inc's ad in 1976 in response to the open letter by Bill Gates

However, almost twenty years after writing that open letter like a Money bull, Bill Gates had a life-changing experience that catalysed his transformation into a Knowledge bull.

Gates had already become the world's richest man and was on a visit to Africa when he saw children dying in hospitals due to tuberculosis, as their parents couldn't even afford basic medicines.

The experience shook Gates, who then decided to pledge a substantial portion of his wealth to the betterment of the world.[11]

The Bill and Melinda Gates Foundation, a charity organisation funded and founded by Bill Gates, with a total endowment of US$ 44.3 billion[12], currently occupies the top spot in the world in terms of funds available at their disposal.

The Gates Foundation works primarily in the areas of healthcare, poverty, water, sanitation and education, and has been recognised for saving millions of lives around the world.

In 2008, Bill Gates withdrew himself from an active role at Microsoft to devote more time to the Gates Foundation.

Gates also eventually announced that he would donate 95 per cent of his wealth to the work of *lok kalyanam*.

In June 2010, Bill Gates, along with the other richest person of the world, Warren Buffet, started 'The Giving Pledge' campaign. The campaign is to encourage wealthy people around the world to commit a substantial portion of their wealth to philanthropic causes. From India, eminent industrialists such as Azim Premji (Founder of Wipro), Kiran Mazumdar-Shaw (founder of Biocon) and Nanadan Nil ani (Co-founder of Infosys) along with his wife Rohini Nil ani have committed their wealth under 'The Giving Pledge'. Particularly, the Nil anis have recently announced that they are going to donate half of their wealth to charitable causes.

It is worth noting that Apple Inc., which published that ad in 1976 offering its interpreters for free, almost exchanged its altruistic position with the man who once wrote that open letter demanding his royalties.

In contrast to Microsoft, Apple Inc. has featured among the least charitable companies in the US.[13] In fact, it did not even have a charitable arm until the year 2011.[14] Steve Jobs believed that creating better-quality products for the people was equivalent to philanthropy, perhaps an indication that there were certain anti-fluid elements in Jobs' personality too.

Incidentally, once Tim Cook took over Apple's leadership in 2011, a shift in the company's approach was seen. As a result, in the past few years, Apple's contribution to charity has increased significantly. In his personal capacity too, Cook has publicly pledged his entire US$ 800 million fortune to the greater good.[15]

***

I want to end this chapter by presenting the journey of an inspiring IIT alumnus named Manu Prakash, who not only refused to walk on the hidden track but also excelled in following the principle of *lok kalyanam*.

Manu Prakash broke the classic IIT-IIM mould, under the grip of which a large number of IIT aspirants enter the coveted engineering institutes with the preconceived idea of following up their engineering degree with a management degree (from business schools such as IIMs). Their dream is to work in business consulting or finance-related jobs.

In many such cases, the students see the visible-track IIT degree as a stepping stone, often not engaging deeply with the curriculum. The hidden tunnel, which could lead them to the doors of business schools or corporate jobs, is getting dug nonstop.

Manu Prakash gained a Bachelor of Technology in Computer Science from IIT, Kanpur (1998–2002),[16] then pursued his masters in applied physics and an interdisciplinary PhD in media arts and sciences, both from the Massachusetts Institute of Technology (MIT), USA.

If one follows the journey of Manu Prakash, who has chosen an academic career, it seems that he has always kept the principles of *lok kalyanam* right at the top.

Born in the year 1980, Manu Prakash became assistant professor at Stanford University's Department of Bioengineering at the young age of thirty-one.

It was at Stanford that he and his team invented a microscope that had a foldable body made out of paper. Manu Prakash called his invention Foldscope,[17] but it is also popularly called the one-dollar microscope because of its incredibly cheap price.

The inspiration to invent Foldscope came through his desire to bring an affordable microscope to the remotest and poorest areas of the world, where in the absence of an expensive microscope many fatal diseases go undiagnosed.

Incidentally, Foldscope was partially funded by the Gates Foundation, which gave a US$ 100,000 grant to Manu Prakash's lab in 2012.[18]

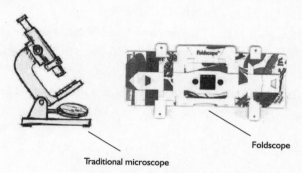

Traditional microscope

Foldscope

Foldscope: a foldable microscope costing $1 (roughly 65 Indian rupees) invented by IITian Manu Prakash

Manu Prakash, who beautifully combined the fields of biology and physics and chose to walk the path of *lok kalyanam*, reflects the true power of a fluid mind. As of 2018, Manu Prakash had thirteen patents to his name (in addition to twenty-one applications that were in patent pending stage).[19]

In 2016, Manu Prakash came up with another remarkable invention, which he called Paperfuge.[20] Paperfuge is a simple paper-and-thread-based yo-yo-like device, which can separate a fluid sample (which is normally done in a laboratory by a giant washing-machine-like device called a centrifuge).

While a lab centrifuge costs thousands of dollars, weighs several kilograms and requires electricity to run, Paperfuge requires just 20 cents-worth (12 paisa) of material, weighs about 20 grams and requires no electricity to run.

In the invention of Paperfuge, Manu Prakash was strongly supported by his team member Saad Bhamla, a postdoctoral fellow then and now an assistant professor himself. Saad Bhamla, a bachelor of technology in chemical engineering from IIT, Madras, and PhD in chemical engineering from Stanford University,[21] also works 'at the interfaces between [various disciplinary] fields', in the words of Moerner, Nobel Prize winner in Chemistry (2014).[22]

Again, both Manu Prakash and Saad Bhamla were driven by the desire to bring an affordable centrifuge to help the world's poorest.

India needs more engineers like Manu Prakash and Saad Bhamla.

'I Am Sick Of This Country'

'I'm sick of this country!' The middle-aged woman finally revealed her true feelings for India to the younger woman standing behind her. I was somewhere behind the younger woman, listening to their verbal confrontation. We were part of the slow-moving immigration queue at the Delhi airport, waiting to catch our respective international flights. I was flying to the UK and, as her red passport revealed, so was the posh-looking middle-aged woman.

It all started when the younger woman requested the woman in front to keep moving. The lady was consciously moving slowly and there seemed to be at least a three-person gap between her and the person in front, which seemed to have irked the younger woman.

At first the woman in front totally ignored the younger one's request, but had an outburst when the younger woman repeated herself.

'Ah! People here don't even have the concept of personal space,' the middle-aged woman spoke in a bitter tone without turning her head.

'There is enough room in front of you, so can you please keep moving? Can you not see that people have squashed up due to lack of space?' the younger woman replied, in a slightly raised voice, pointing to the back of the queue.

'You guys don't know how to even queue. Good that you are visiting a foreign country. At least you will learn how to queue,' the woman turned towards the younger one and continued in her acerbic tone.

'This is not how you queue, and why are you assuming that I have not lived outside? And, by the way, if you find this place so repulsive, why don't you leave?' The young lady, who wore an Indian attire and had an Indian passport, was now clearly riled up.

'That is exactly what I am doing. Look at the dirt and filth around. I'm sick of this country!'

Listening to what the elder woman said about India, one might assume that she must be of foreign origin; however, this was certainly not the case. The woman, although carried the red British passport, was clearly of Indian origin. In fact, it seemed quite probable that she could have very well lived in India for a couple of decades before moving to England. Yet she had now totally disassociated herself from her Indian identity.

***

If one has travelled enough, internationally, it is not difficult to encounter somebody of Indian origin similar to the middle-aged woman from the Delhi airport incident—ones who deliberately flaunt a differently-coloured passport and make sure to speak loudly enough in an acquired accent for everyone around to know that they are not one of them. In fact, if such a person happens to be on a smaller domestic flight, the entire plane comes to know that he is not an Indian—his gestures, mannerisms, words, all would try hard to point out that he is different—that now, he is part of a culture or a country that is superior.

In fact, when such a person visits India, his b aviour often finds encouragement from a large section of the local population, who give such people added attention.

This is largely because many from the local side fear, on a subconscious level, that their Indian identity is somewhat inferior.

Incidentally, the young lady standing right b ind the woman had no such inferior feelings about her identity and hence she did not take the verbal attack quietly. It was almost exactly like what Mahatma Gandhi did when he was asked to leave the first-class compartment in South Africa on the pretext that he was not white skinned. He did not take it quietly. He protested to the police officers, because he was not ashamed of who he was and where he came from. If he had left quietly, he wouldn't have been thrown out of the train.

If we translate the airport incident into our understanding of the current Indian education system, we would realise it is also largely plagued with such feelings of superiority and inferiority.

As our current education model is almost entirely imported from the West, the West som ow seems superior. English, as the medium of learning, carries that superior connotation. And with most of the leading characters of all the disciplines (those who laid the foundation of physics, chemistry, math, biology, economics, etc.) not originating from India, the entire world of learning seems alien to the young mind. This mind often lacks confidence and adopts rote learning to master this alien world, and in the process is often tempted to throw away its Indian identity.

Here, I want to make it clear that by no means am I making a jingoistic call to give up on English or to denounce Western education; what I am saying is to expand your learning and identify that your Indian identity also has great things to offer. It is not inferior in any way whatsoever.

Perhaps this is exactly how the younger woman from the airport incident or Mahatma Gandhi felt—open-hearted to embrace what the world had to offer and yet comfortable with who they were.

It is only when one pierces the boundaries of identity, race, religion, colour and country that true learning can happen.

And only when one reaches this fluid state, does one realise that human knowledge is circulatory. The world has been benefited not by knowledge originating from one single country or one single race, but by the combined intelligence of all, spread over thousands of years.

The Power Of Combined Fluidity

There have been several nights when, way past midnight, in order to unwind and think in peace, I drive aimlessly on the wide roads of what is now known as Lutyens' Delhi. Of late, on many of these nights, I drive towards the President's house (Rashtrapati Bhavan) and quietly park myself right between the two imposing blocks at its entrance for a little while, before driving down slowly the Rajpath,[1] towards the India Gate.

The drive brings out mixed emotions in me. On one hand, I am deeply impressed by the magnanimity of the plan, grandness of the President's house and the India Gate, and the fact that I am driving on the road where the annual Republic Day parade takes place. On the other hand, I am a little embarrassed to think that the so-called India Gate and our president's residence were both designed and built by the very British who once enslaved my country. And when such thoughts occur, the structures start appearing to me as symbols of tyranny and colonialism.

It was one such night that compelled me to research the origin of these structures. The exercise transformed my fixed understanding and revealed to me the power of combined fluidity.

Most of us would know that the project of the President's house was taken up by the British to house their viceroy, the governor general—their highest ruling officer for India. It was the year 1911 and the British had decided to shift the capital of India from Calcutta (now Kolkata) to Delhi. It was due to this very move that the idea of building a newer Delhi came about.

The task of building this newer Delhi eventually came to the desk of two leading British architects—Edwin Lutyens and Herbert Baker.

The idea was clear—the Viceroy's House was to be the nerve centre of this new Delhi. It was an opportunity for the British to display their imperialistic domination to the world. This was, perhaps, the reason it eventually became the largest single-residence project the world has ever seen. As we now know, it contains 340 rooms. The India Gate, which stands right at the far end of Rajpath facing the President's house, was initially conceived as its giant gateway—symbolically, the gateway to India. It was to dazzle all those key dignitaries who would come to visit the Viceroy's house, by making them enter through the huge arched India Gate. As they would move along the 2.5-kilometre-long Kingsway,[2] their eyes transfixed on the colossal Viceroy's residence, they would have no chance to escape being completely in awe of British superiority.[3]

Incidentally, Edwin Lutyens, almost like that posh middle-aged woman from the Delhi airport, did not initially think much of traditional Indian architecture. He dismissed it by calling it 'piffle' (nonsense) and declaring:

> I do not believe there is any real Indian architecture at all, or any great tradition...[4]

As idiotic as it may sound today, Lutyens considered the Taj Mahal to be 'wonderful but not architecture'.

After the 1857 revolt, the British wanted to show sensitivity towards the feelings of the local population, and hence Lutyens was asked to incorporate elements from Indian architecture into the planned new capital, against which he strongly protested with the following words:

They want me to Hindoo, Hindon't I say...[5]

Incidentally, Lutyens eventually agreed to include Indian components in his design. But if we look at his final result, we realise that the architectural knowledge that Lutyens pompously thought was his creation was not his, but had been gathered by the human race over centuries.

It was his arrogance that confined Lutyens to the prison of knowledge inside the little box of race and country, and made him believe that whatever was being created through him was a sign of the superiority of himself, his race and his country. This, sadly for him, was never the case.

If we stand beneath the India Gate and look upward, we cannot avoid being impressed by its 138-feet-high and 30-feet-wide arch. However, this arch-based gate structure is not at all the invention of the British.

Based on the 'triumphal arch' architectural style, the twentieth-century India Gate is starkly similar to the nineteenth-century Arc de Triomphe, situated in Paris, France.

However, the giant archway-gate style is also not a French invention, but was heavily inspired by the Roman Arch of Titus, which was built in the first century.

In fact, the term 'triumphal arch' was given to this style because the Romans initially had giant arched gates at the entrance of their cities, through which the Roman army paraded into the city after their triumphs over their enemies. During these parades, the gate was usually decorated with flowers and trophies as a symbol of victory, which eventually became permanent fixtures when such arch gates were recreated.

In later centuries, the archway gate became a symbol of

domination and a tool for propaganda, and several such projects were undertaken by the respective rulers of various countries.

Interestingly, Adolf Hitler had plans to build what would have been the world's largest triumphal arch in Berlin. Planned to be 550-feet-tall, it would have been at least five times taller than the India Gate.

Continuing with the journey of the triumphal arch, it seems that the Romans were not the inventors of these arches either, but took inspiration from other such gateway structures that had already been in existence in older civilisations.

One such gateway was the Ishtar Gate, which was built almost 700 years before the Roman arches, in Babylon in the Mesopotamian region (present-day Iraq). Due to the lack of availability of data, one can only conclude that perhaps the Ishtar Gate would also have been the result of knowledge drawn from various other ancient civilisations.

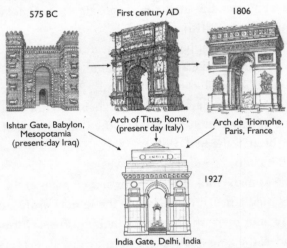

Combined intelligence journey of India Gate

Thankfully, by the time Edwin Lutyens finalised the design of the India Gate, he had realised that knowledge doesn't have a country, race or religion. And now with the boundaries demolished, his eyes also started appreciating traditional Indian architecture, as confirmed by his own statement:

East and West can and do meet, with mutual respect and affection.[6]

He demonstrated his fluidity by incorporating Indian elements into the final design, and the result was magnificent. For the first time, a triumphal arch had a dome over its top. Lutyens had taken this element from third-century-BC Buddhist stupa structures built by King Ashoka in Sanchi, a small, ancient town of central India. The canopy structure, which stood just beside the India Gate, took the inspiration for its roof from the seventh-century Shore Temple situated in the Mahabalipuram city of Tamil Nadu.

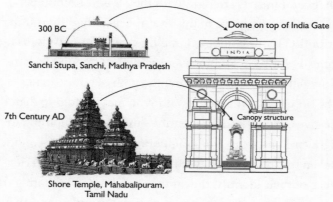

India Gate: Elements inspired from Indian architecture

If we analyse the 2500-year-odd journey of the India Gate, we realise that not one country or race can lay a singular claim over its design—the ones who created its versions can only take credit for leaving their imprints on the unified knowledge, which eventually belongs to the entire world.

This book, in its initial chapters, highlighted the example of Leonardo da Vinci—considered to be one of the greatest minds human civilisation has ever produced. His achievements have almost turned da Vinci into a demi-god, due to which many assume that he was a genius who never needed to rely on others. This tendency often causes us to assume that Leonardo da Vinci or geniuses like him are far above the requirement of shaping their intelligence, and that the results achieved by them are impossible to emulate.

I want to end this book by highlighting those aspects of Leonardo da Vinci that confirm that brilliant minds like him are also the product of the unified nature of knowledge.

My final example has two purposes:

The first purpose is clearly to stress that no matter how extraordinary a fluid mind is, it only remains extraordinary when it combines its strength with the other fluid minds.

The second purpose of this example is to highlight India's contribution to the combined intelligence of human civilisation, specifically for those millions and millions of young Indians who are either currently walking the path of education or will be doing so in the future, and who may be told to disrobe themselves of their Indian identity—that there is nothing to look inward and learn from this country. If ever their confidence is shaken by anyone or if ever they are made to feel inferior because of their identity, they must spend time meditating over this particular example and several such examples, and they may soon realise how crucial they are for the advancement of human civilisation.

Finally, the example is for that woman from the airport, to request that she not consider the Indian elements of her identity to be inferior, and to salute that girl who embraced all aspects of her identity with pride.

**

At the beginning of this book, we discussed the fifteenth-century fluid thinker Leonardo da Vinci and highlighted his various masterpieces.

Here, I want to discuss his one particular iconic creation that wasn't mentioned in the initial chapters.

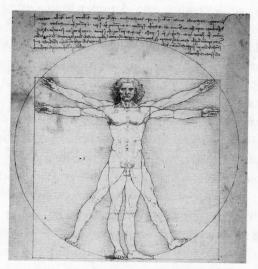

Vitruvian Man by Leonardo da Vinci, created around 1490

The Vitruvian Man, as it is famously called, is considered to be the ultimate symbolic representation of the Renaissance period and one of the finest handiworks of da Vinci. The drawing is a beautiful convergence of artistic, scientific and mathematical knowledge. The Vitruvian Man basically represents a perfectly physically proportionate man. That is, if there were to be a perfect man, his precise measurements would be those possessed by the Vitruvian Man (for example, the size of his fingers, length of his head, width of his shoulders, etc. are all proportionate to each other).

As most people would know, the idea of the Vitruvian Man was not originally Leonardo da Vinci's.

A first-century-BC Roman architect and engineer, Marcus

Vitruvius Pollio (popularly known simply as Vitruvius), developed the idea of a perfectly proportionate man. Hence, Leonardo named his drawing after Vitruvius, as he was reproducing the proportions given by the Roman. It is important to note that da Vinci did not entirely follow the proportions given by Vitruvius while creating The Vitruvian Man. Out of roughly around twenty-two measurements noted by Vitruvius, Leonardo da Vinci takes only less than half and combines them with his self-devised specifications of human physical proportions to create the iconic image.

Vitruvius, who is also often called the first architect of the world, is famous for his pioneering text on architecture, *De architectura*[7]—the only surviving book from the ancient Roman period on architecture, which was eventually rediscovered in the fifteenth century. Its contents formed a strong foundation for the likes of Leonardo da Vinci and Michelangelo to base their creations.

Considered to be written around 15–30 BC, *De architectura*, comprising ten brief books, essentially contains principles of building design and town planning, including city drainage and water systems.

Book IV (chapters 3–8) of *De architectura* explains how a theatre should be designed. The basic design of an amphitheatre—with semi-circular seating in front of the stage and rows of seats increasing in height—that we see all around us, is found in the chapter on theatre design in the 2000-year-old *De architectura*.

Some of the chapters of the book are quite compr ensive, dealing with the foundation of a building, its flooring, colouring, types of individual residences and even rainwater management.

Interestingly, *De architectura* also contains chapters on military equipment, sundials, water clocks, planetary mechanisms and even the fundamentals of machines.

In fact, *De architectura* played a pivotal role in Leonardo's fluid ventures. It was *De architectura* that inspired the brilliant mind to conceive bridge designs, military tanks, water mills, etc., apart from the famous Vitruvian Man.

It was in Book III, Chapter 1, Symmetry: In Temples and The Human Body of *De architectura* that Vitruvius elaborates on the proportions of a perfect man.

According to Vitruvius, the navel of such a man is at the centre of his body,[8] and if a circle is drawn from this centre with the arms and legs stretched, the tips of the fingers and toes would touch the circumference of the circle. Not only that, if a square is drawn, they would touch the boundaries of the square too. In fact, once extended fully, the length of the stretched arms is equal to the height of a perfectly proportionate man. And, as per Vitruvius, this length is equivalent to ten heads when the head is measured 'from the chin to the top of the for ead and the lowest root of the hair'.

It is commonly understood that the idea of a perfectly proportioned man was originally and exclusively that of Vitruvius, which is actually not the case. Indeed, Vitruvius himself records this fact immediately after revealing the idea of the 'well-shaped man':

> …it was by employing them [symmetrical proportions] that the famous painters and sculptors of antiquity attained to great and endless renown. (p 72, Book III, *Des Architectura*).

And, as unbelievable as it may sound, one such place where the extensive measurements of a perfectly proportionate human body are found recorded, in all probability before *Des Architectura*, is none other than the encyclopedic *Vishnudharmottaram Puranam*.

If you recall, I requested in a previous chapter that you keep the long-named, lesser-known ancient Indian text in memory.

Now is the time to enter back into the fascinating world of *Vishnudharmottaram Puranam* and continue listening to the captivating conversation of King Vajra and Rishi Markandeya.

As mentioned earlier, *Chitra Sutra*, part 3 of the *Puranam* begins with Rishi Markandeya's explanation of the integrative nature of all disciplines and in turn the universe to King Vajra. Almost 100 pages and a few hundred *shloka*s later, Rishi Markandeya begins his detailed discourse on the proportions of human body.

After I submerged myself for days in understanding the concept of a perfect human body, I was overtaken by astonishment on two levels: firstly, the depth in which the proportions of human body were stated in *Vishnudharmottaram Puranam* almost dwarfed the calculations as given by Vitruvius in *Des Architectura*. And secondly, why the *Puranam's* perfect human body measurements are virtually unheard of and un-cited in the public domain. Even the ones who translated the *Puranam* never bring up Vitruvius or *Des Architectura* in their commentaries.

As I went along with my comparisions of *Des Architectura* and *Vishnudharmottaram Puranam*, I realised that one of the key reasons why Markandeya's text could achieve greater depth with his calculations is simply mathematical.

While Vitruvius predominantly uses the length of the face as a unit to measure human body, Markandeya uses a much smaller unit—the width of a single finger, i.e., the entire human body is actually in multiples of the width of a single finger (*angula*). The applicability of smaller measuring unit gives Markandeya the advantage to measure smaller body parts too.

For novices in body sketching, like me, the information that our body is proportionate to the width of a finger is simply astonishing.

I was startled when I tried measuring my own self with the help of my forefinger—the lower lip was found to be equal to the width of the forefinger, the width of the eye equal to three fingers, the height of the ear equal to four fingers, and so on and so forth.

The advantage of using a measuring unit as small as the finger gives Markandeya the freedom to provide measurements of even body parts such as teeth, eyes and even nails. For instance, according to Markandeya, the front teeth of a perfect man are half finger in length. No such depth is reached by Vitruvius.

Another feat that takes Markandeya's explanation to a much advanced level is his mentioning that there are five kinds of perfect men, unlike Vitruvian, who gives the proportions for only one kind.

Rishi Markandeya calls these perfect men (Chapter 36, *shloka*s 8-11):

1. *Hans*
2. *Bhadra*
3. *Malvya*
4. *Ruchak*
5. *Shashak*

As the table below depicts, these perfect men have varied heights (and, accordingly, different body proportions).

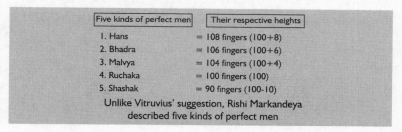

Five kinds of perfect men	Their respective heights
1. Hans	= 108 fingers (100+8)
2. Bhadra	= 106 fingers (100+6)
3. Malvya	= 104 fingers (100+4)
4. Ruchaka	= 100 fingers (100)
5. Shashak	= 90 fingers (100-10)

Unlike Vitruvius' suggestion, Rishi Markandeya described five kinds of perfect men

Out of these five men, according to Rishi Markandeya, the proportions of *Hans* are said to be nearer to perfection.

Hans, the name of the perfect man of Rishi Markandeya, in Sanskrit stands for a mythical bird that is considered to be the finest among all birds. The *hans* bird that appears closest to a swan in its physical appearance is said to have the ability of separating divine nectar (*amrit*) from water.

It is important to note that Rishi Markandeya not only gave the body proportions of these men, but also explained in considerable detail their gestures, postures, expressions, hairstyle, etc. when drawn. For instance, the arms of *Hans* Man should be as strong as the width of the king of serpents (king cobra) with a circle of his curly hair falling between the two eyebrows.

The Vitruvian Man, a depiction of a male body, is often blamed as a symbol of gender bias. Interestingly, in *Vishnudharmottaram Puranam*, along with the five types of perfect men, measurements of five types of perfect women are also given.

For instance, *Hans* Woman's waist needs to be two fingers thinner than that of *Hans* Man, whereas her hips need to be four fingers wider.[9]

As mentioned earlier, Leonardo da Vinci, while drawing The Vitruvian Man, did not follow the words of Vitruvius verbatim. For example, the height of Vitruvian Man is equivalent to the width of 112 fingers whereas the perfect man of Vitruvius translates to be just 96 fingers tall. Interestingly, *Hans* Man with the height of 108 fingers is closer to Leonardo's Vitruvian Man.

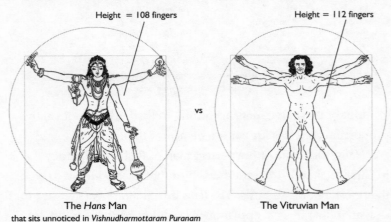

Height = 108 fingers   Height = 112 fingers

vs

The *Hans* Man   The Vitruvian Man
that sits unnoticed in *Vishnudharmottaram Puranam*

The *Hans* Man vs The Vitruvian Man

The above illustration is the concluding one of *Fluid* but perhaps also its most important one. It is truly ironic that while numerous attempts have been made to draw a proportionate man using the measurements of Vitruvius, no such attempt has been made on the proportions given by Rishi Markandeya. As a result, it is still a mystery that how eventually the older-than-2000-year *Hans* Man or *Hans* Woman will look once they are sketched on paper. I produce the comparative drawing with the hope that it inspires millions of current Leonardo da Vincis to finally bring the Indian Vitruvian Man and Woman to life. Yes, millions of da Vincis and not handful because once we are on the path of fluidity we realise that it was da Vinci's innate desire to attempt everything that makes him a genius and not vice versa. Before anything else, da Vinci was a true learner, perhaps as much a disciple of Rishi Markandeya as he was that of Vitruvius. Leonardo da Vinci stood on the shoulders of the giants to combine his fluidity with theirs to eventually become what he was—so should we.

Let's End With Fatima Al-fihri

In 2014, I happened to get invited to the World Innovation Summit for Education (WISE) at Doha. WISE is an international event where educationists from all around the world come together to discuss issues and advancements in the field of education.

On the last day of the summit, a few international delegates received private invites to spend an evening at the headquarters of Al Jazeera media network—the famous Middle Eastern channel which is incidentally owned by Qatar's ruling family. As our minibus entered the heavily-guarded headquarters of Al Jazeera, I could see some nervous faces among us. What added to the nervousness was the fact that hardly any information was divulged on the reason for our invite.

As we later came to know, we were invited to se inputs on the expansion of AJ+ channel. Backed by Al Jazeera, AJ+ produces thought-provoking and educational content with the aim to empower African and Middle Eastern youths.

Although the people at the media house were very hospitable, it didn't help much to reduce the scepticism of the majority among us.

While giving us the inside tour, our hosts took us into one of the halls that had a huge wall-to-wall poster with the following headline:

Fatima al-Fihri

The woman who founded the world's oldest
existing university

The poster informed that in the year 859, almost 1200 years ago, Fatima, after the death of her father and brother, used her entire wealth to start the University of Al Quaraouiyine in Fes, Morocco.

The information sounded quite unbelievable to almost all of us. For instance, I had always presumed that my almost-1000-year-old university (Oxford) was the oldest existing university in the world.

Although we remained quiet, it was obvious that no one actually believed the poster to be true. Even the fact that this feat is recorded in the Guinness book of world records didn't do much to change our hardened perceptions.

That night, Fatima al-Fihri and her life occupied the central stage during our dinner conversation. For many, it was impossible to come to terms that at the time when women's rights were not even a topic of contention in Europe, a ninth-century Middle Eastern woman had the courage and freedom to start a university.

Most notably, this was not some ordinary dinner conversation but the one where everyone was supposed to be an expert in the field of education.

It was during that dinner when the idea of *Fluid* came into being.

I leave you to ponder over what it would have taken the people on that night to look at Fatima al-Fihri's achievements in true light.

Acknowledgements

Fluid, in its current shape and form, would not have been possible without the friends I made at Oxford. We all come from different backgrounds, have studied at different departments, yet, we spent hundreds of nights discussing contrasting topics ranging from AI to the Renaissance to gender equality to the threats of antibiotics to the death penalty to Marxism. Proudly, every time we managed to end our discussions without getting into fisticuffs.

There is little doubt that our interaction has compelled me to go beyond the comfort zone of my own field. It has pushed me to read books I wouldn't normally read. It has forced me to engage with alternative viewpoints. And above all, remain in a Zen-like state even if I was in strong disagreement.

To the everlasting fluid friendships.

It was December 2016. The idea of *Fluid* had been with me for quite some time but I wasn't able to get myself together sufficiently to begin the writing marathon. And then two major things happened.

First, out of sheer luck, the legendary writer and poet, Javed Akhtar, visited our house in Delhi. It was our usual diverse 'Oxford gang' (as he terms us), which was then joined by the writer of some of the most iconic Bollywood films. During the evening, which lasted until 2 am, he mesmerised us by his depth of sociocultural, political and scientific understanding. I could now see why his films are exceptional displays of fantasy and reality. For me, it was a fluid mind playing right in front of me. Before he brought the night to an end, he entered my study and unknowingly flipped through a very early version of this book. His visit brought a volcanic amount of energy to my writing and I ended up spending almost all of 2017 in my study writing *Fluid*.

To the inspiring legend.

A couple of days after that captivating evening, I left for Auroville, the enigmatic coastal town which adjoins Puducherry in southern India. The month I spent in Auroville has been life-changing. I hardly read any books, yet, I learned things I hadn't learnt previously in my life. Here, nature itself was my teacher. Walking for hours on the dusty trails of Auroville provided me the reflective space to plan the initial plot of *Fluid*. It was because of Auroville and the people I interacted with that I decided that *Fluid* should definitively convey the idea that education is not only about books, degrees and mind.

To the Auroville energy.

Once I was back from Auroville, it was all about writing non-stop. Although one could see me writing all alone in my study, I was not actually alone. I had the company of Anoushka Shankhar's divine sitar. There were times when the audio of her performances played for days on a loop. Whenever I got stuck, the heavenly melody blossomed new ideas. I wish her sitar plays until eternity. Accompanying the sitar was mridanga being played by the maestro, Umayalpuram Sivaraman. Way past midnight when everything slept, the thumping of mridanga kept me focused.

To the angelic instruments that accompanied me.

I was quite particular that *Fluid* gets read and understood by a schoolgoer. Hence, I must thank Navyasara, my thirteen-year-old daughter for ensuring that I follow a story-like narrative. I want to acknowledge everyone who read *Fluid* during its creation and provided priceless inputs. As ideal as it would have been for a topic like this, the readers ranged from thirteen-year-olds to seventy-year-olds. I want to specifically mention Manav Bhushan, Nupur Gupta, Sarah Iqbal, Mr Arun Mirchandani and my dad for being with me through the entire process right from patiently going through the drafts umpteen times, fiercely suggesting changes and of course, weeding out many of my collection of seventy-odd titles.

However, the woman who was once a banker in England but now working in India to further the boundaries of how working women's wellness should be tackled, an Oxford alum and, of course, my best friend and beloved wife, Pooja, has played the most important role in this whole journey. She has not only helped me lay *Fluid* brick-by-brick but also made sure that I maintained the balance between scholarly rigour and free-spirited instincts.

To all those who nurtured *Fluid* in its unbound state.

Actually, *Fluid* wouldn't have been called by this name but for a last minute meeting with prodigious historian, artist and a dear friend, Moonis Ijlal. When I met Moonis, the manuscript was almost ready to go into print with a different title. It took him ten minutes to give me a hundred reasons for why what I had written could not be called anything other than *Fluid*. I happened to remember Bruce Lee's famous quote on being like water. When I came home and saw Lee speak, no doubt remained regarding the title.

To Moonis for naming *Fluid*.

If the cover and extended communication of *Fluid* look cool, it is all the handiwork of exemplary designer, Ibrahim Rayintakath.

Fluid is fortunate to begin with Malvina Reynolds' song *Little Boxes*. Heartfelt thanks to Malvina's daughter Nancy Schimmel for kindly allowing *Little Boxes* to be associated with *Fluid*.

I have to specially thank my dearest friend, Sarah Iqbal, who like Malvina Reynolds is not only a melodious singer but also a doctorate in Chemistry from Oxford. Sarah not only encouraged me to write on fluidity of disciplines but also acted as a true ambassador by mentioning her 'favourite' 'upcoming book' on cross-disciplinarity to as many people she came across as possible.

To Sarah for being the rock solid anchor and true motivator.

Finally, *Fluid* would have remained tucked inside my study if my publisher, Wisdom Tree, hadn't drawn it out with mighty force. Although this is my first book with the publication house, I have almost been treated like a star. I was humbled to hear that Shobit Arya, founder of Wisdom Tree, who himself happens to be a writer, considers *Fluid* to be 'groundbreaking and a mandatory read for every young mind'. Shobit considered the project so crucial that he not only wore the editorial hat but also dedicated countless hours in ensuring that every key element of the book publication and distribution puzzle is in its precise place.

To the wisdom of Shobit.

If you are reading *Fluid*, it is clear that there are enlightened souls who are spreading the good word.

Fluid would not become the kind of revolution it can be without your contribution. Because a sea only gathers its invincibility from hundreds of streams, which selflessly submerge themselves in it. Without the rivers, there would be no life in the oceans.

To everyone: Thank you.

Notes And References

Let's Start With Malvina Reynolds

1. Teez, M and Cabrera, N. (2014) [Internet] La Peña Mural 1. Malvina Reynolds. Available from: <http://scalar.usc.edu/works/la-pea-mural-/malvina-reynolds.history> [Accessed 5 February 2017].

Anti-fluid

Scientists Only Do Science

1. Dorm l, D. (2017) [Internet] Why Apple Park is Steve Jobs' final project. Available from: <https://www.cultofmac.com/481819/apple-park-steve-jobss-final-project/> [Accessed 20 May 2017].
2. 9TO5MAC (2017) [Internet] Apple Park Stories. Available from: https://9to5mac.com/guides/apple-park/ [Accessed 21 October 2017].
3. Potuck, M. (2017) [Internet] Report breaks down cost of $5B Apple Park, $427M spaceship, $180M theater, $113M parking structures, and more. Available from: https://9to5mac.com/2017/10/04/apple-park-cost-breakdown-details/ [Accessed 21 October 2017].
4. Robinson, A. (2002) [Internet] A grouse for Mr Bigwiz. Available from: https://www.timeshighereducation.com/features/a-grouse-for-mr-bigwiz/171012.article [Accessed 16 February 2017].

Businessmen Only Do Business

1. *Adarsh* (ideal) *gram* (village) is the Sanskrit term for ideal village, also popularly termed 'model village' in India. A model village, in a simpler sense, means a village which not only has basic development infrastructure such as water, sanitation, roads, electricity, health centre, school, etc. (which is otherwise lacking in several villages in India) but often uses

environmentally friendly frameworks to achieve these. It also aims to generate employment locally to prevent urban migration.

Anti-fluidity: The Wrong Turn In Our Education

1. Listed as one of the 100 books that influenced Western public discourse since the end of World War II. *The Times* (2008) The hundred most influential books since the war. *The Times*. London.
2. Snow, CP (1960:1) The Two Cultures and the Scientific Revolution. Cambridge, Cambridge University Press.
3. ibid., p. 2.
4. ibid. p. 4.
5. The ribosome is part of a plant or animal cell outside its nucleus.
6. THE TELEGRAPH, INDIA (2015) [Internet] Not everything that sounds scientific is science. That is a worldwide problem—in India it is more widespread. Available from: https://www.telegraphindia.com/1151227/jsp/7days/story_60563.jsp [Accessed 11 January 2016].
7. I address the topic of specialists in greater detail in later chapters.

Artists Doing Science

1. Iezzi, T. (2015) [Internet] Neil deGrasse Tyson Stomps the Notion of Left vs. Right Brain, Salutes Jon Stewart, and Explains the Soul of Creativity. Available from: https://www.fastcompany.com/3045459/neil-degrasse-tyson-stomps-the-notion-of-left-right-brain-salutes-jon-stewart-and-explains-t [Accessed 11 February 2017].
2. Parker-pope, T. (2008) [Internet] The Truth About the Spinning Dancer. Available from: https://well.blogs.nytimes.com/2008/04/28/the-truth-about-the-spinning-dancer/ [Accessed 11 February 2017].
3. Bulent, A. (2013). [Internet] Leonardo's Bridge: Part 2. A Bridge for the Sultan. *National Geographic Voice*. Available from: https://voices.nationalgeographic.org/2013/01/22/leonardos-bridge-part-2-the-bridge-for-the-sultan/ [Accessed 11 February 2017].
4. Institut de France, Paris.
5. Leonardo da Vinci carried out over 30 dissections during 1510 and 1511, and created over 240 anatomical drawings supported by detailed description of the structure and functioning of the respective organs.
6. Furness, H. (2013) [Internet] Leonardo da Vinci was right all along, new medical scans show. Available from: http://www.telegraph.co.uk/culture/theatre/edinburgh-festival/9923336/Leonardo-da-Vinci-was-right-all-along-new-medical-scans-show.html [Accessed 11 March 2017].
7. Especially the ones who understand these concepts on a superficial level.
8. Gonzalez, BH. & Kuenzi, JJ. (2012) [Internet] Science, Technology, Engineering, and Mathematics (STEM) Education: A Primer. Available from: https://fas.org/sgp/crs/misc/R42642.pdf [Accessed 4 June 2015].

9.   Garner, R. (2014) [Internet] Education Secretary Nicky Morgan tells teenagers: Want to keep your options open? Then do science. Available from: http://www.independent.co.uk/news/education/education-news/education-secretary-nicky-morgan-tells-teenagers-if-you-want-a-job-drop-humanities-9852316.html [Accessed 15 July 2015].

10. ibid. [Accessed 15 October 2017].

11. For instance, the initiative of 'STEM to STEAM' (exploring the contribution of arts and design in STEM areas) promoted by the Rhode Island School of Design (source: http://stemtosteam.org/).

12. Durant, W. (1953) *The Renaissance: A History of Civilization in Italy from 1304-1576 A.D.* Berkeley, Simon and Schuster.

13. Cunningham, LS; Reich, JJ & Fichner-Rathus, L. *Culture and Values: A Survey of the Humanities*, Vol. 2. Boston, Wadsworth, p. 421.

14. Orville Wright (1871–1948) and Wilbur Wright (1867–1912), American aviation pioneers.

15. William Blake (1757–1827), poet, painter and printmaker.

16. Goethe, JW. (1882) *The Autobiography of Goethe: Truth and Poetry from My Own Life*, 2 vols. John Oxenford (trans). London, George Bell.

17. There is no English word that can truly convey the meaning of the Sanskrit word *abhigyan*. The closest translation is 'new knowledge' or 'new and higher awareness'. Although the first English translation of the play in the late eighteenth century was titled *Sacontala or The Fatal Ring*, the correct translation of *Abhigyan Shakuntalam* should be 'the new and higher knowledge about Shakuntala' or 'the new awareness about Shakuntala'.

18. 'A great poet' or 'the poet among poets'.

19. The exact period of Kalidas' life cannot be mentioned with certainty as there is a profuse lack of unanimity among historians and biographers. He is considered to have lived anywhere between 500 BC and 300 AD.

20. Freeman, IA. (2014) *Seeds of Revolution: A Collection of Axioms, Passages and Proverbs*, Vol. 1. Bloomington, iUniverse.

21. Miller, GL. Introduction. In Goethe, JW. (2009) [originally 1790] *The Metamorphosis of Plants*. Cambridge, Massachusetts, The MIT Press, p. xvi.

22. The duchy of Saxe-Weimar-Eisenach (a large province comprising several small German cities and the surrounding region) was ruled by Duke Charles Augustus between 1758 and 1828. The Duke employed Goethe as a poet, and he in turn brought several other scholars and laid the foundation of an intellectual movement famously known as Weimar Classicism.

23. Brady, RH. (1987) Form and Cause in Goethe's Morphology. In Amrine F, Zucker FJ, Wheeler H (eds) *Goethe and the Sciences: A Reappraisal*. Boston Studies in the Philosophy of Science, Vol. 97. Springer, Dordrecht.

24. Commonly known as *kaner* in India and oleander elsewhere, it is one of the most frequently planted shrubs along the roadside in India. Oleander is the

official flower of the city of Hiroshima, as it was the first to bloom after the atomic bombing of the city in 1945. *Nerium indicum* or *Nerium oleander* is the botanical name of *kaner*.

25. Miller, GL. Introduction. In Goethe, JW. (2009) [originally 1790] *The Metamorphosis of Plants*. Cambridge, Massachusetts, The MIT Press, p. xxiv.

26. ibid. p. xxiii.

27. Portor, LS. (1917) *The Greatest Books in the World: Interpretative Studies*. Chautauqua, NY, Chautauqua Press, p. 82.

28. Nash, ML. (1963) [Internet] The Man Who Invented Tomorrow. *Boy's Life Magazine*. May 1963, pp. 18-21. Available from: https://teslauniverse.com/nikola-tesla/articles/man-who-invented-tomorrow [Accessed 15 October 2017].

Scientists Doing Arts

1. Raman, CV & Kumar, S. (1920) Musical Drums with Harmonic Overtones. *Nature*. Vol. 104, pp. 500-501. doi: 10.1038/104500a0.

2. Raman, CV. (1934). The Indian musical drums. *Proceedings of the Indian Academy of Sciences*. Vol. 1, pp. 179–188.

3. After attaining his Nobel Prize in 1930, Raman founded the Indian Academy of Sciences, a non-profit research organisation, and remained its president until he died in 1970.

4. The branch of physics that studies sound.

5. Raman, CV & Kumar, S. (1920) Musical Drums with Harmonic Overtones. *Nature*. Vol. 104, p. 453. doi: 10.1038/104500a0.

6. Conard, NJ; Malina, M & Münzel, SC. (2009) New Flutes Document the Earliest Musical Tradition in Southwestern Germany. *Nature*. Vol. 460, pp. 737–40. doi:10.1038/nature08169.

7. Bamboo in Hindi is called *bans*. Hence, the Indian flute, which is made from bamboo, is justly called *Bansuri* (*bans+sur*)—a piece of bamboo that is melodious.

8. Creating a flute can be a great learning experience and would bring you closer to both arts and sciences. For those interested, a compr ensive step-by-step guide can be found at: https://www.tapatalk.com/groups/paleoplanet69529/bansuri-build-along-t36761.html.

9. progenitors = creators

10. The Ajanta Caves are known to have been built in two phases: the first set of caves is dated between 200BC and 100AD, and the second is dated between 400AD and 600AD.

11. In a way, a mridanga doesn't have a right side or a left side. Between the two drumheads, the narrower drumhead is the one that produces harmonic overtones, and as majority of people are right-handers, this side is facing the right-hand palm of the player. A left-handed player would invert this and play the narrower drumhead with his left-hand palm and fingers.

Businessmen Doing Arts And Sciences

1. CNN (2018) [Internet] Apple is leading the race to $1 trillion. Available from: http://money.cnn.com/2018/02/27/investing/apple-google-amazon-microsoft-trillion-dollar-market-value/index.html [Accessed 28 February 2018].

2. Macrotrends (2018) Coca-Cola Market Cap History (KO). Available from: http://www.macrotrends.net/stocks/charts/KO/market-cap/coca-cola-co-market-cap-history [Accessed 23 April 2018].

3. FE Online (2018) [Internet] India's 1st $100 billion company. Available from: https://www.financialexpress.com/market/indias-1st-100-billion-company-history-created-tcs-becomes-nations-biggest-company-by-market-cap/1142034/ [Accessed 24 April 2018].

4. Chakraborty, S & Modak, S. (2017) [Internet] HDFC Bank, SBI now among top 50 most-valued global banks. Available from: http://www.business-standard.com/article/finance/hdfc-bank-sbi-now-among-top-50-most-valued-global-banks-115011700545_1.html [Accessed 02 August 2017].

5. Pogue, D. (2007) [Internet] The iPhone Matches Most of Its Hype. *New York Times*. 27 June 2007. Available from: http://www.nytimes.com/2007/06/27/technology/circuits/27pogue.html [Accessed 02 August 2017].

6. Eadicicco, L; Peckham, M; Fitzpatrick, A; Pullen, PJ; Luckerson, V & Howorth, C. (2007) [Internet] The 50 Most Influential Gadgets of All Time. Available from: http://time.com/4309573/most-influential-gadgets/ [Accessed 02 August 2017].

7. At the release of the first iPhone model on 29 June 2007, a controversy broke in which LG claimed that Apple's iPhone was a copy of its model, Prada, photos of which had been circulating in public domain since January 2007. Prada's sale started a month prior to that of the iPhone.

8. Starting with 2007's first-generation iPhone to iPhone X, which was presented to the world in the latter half of 2017, there have been eighteen models of iPhone.

9. Muelle, CM. (2013) [Internet] The History of Kindergarten: From Germany to the United States. Available from: http://digitalcommons.fiu.edu/cgi/viewcontent.cgi?article=1110&context=sferc [Accessed 03 September 2017].

10. Hence, that popular egg-shaped chocolate brand targeted at children is called Kinder Joy.

11. Wright, FL. (1957) *A Testament*. New York, Horizon Press, pp. 19–20.

12. Hinman, K. (2017) [Internet] America's Greatest Work of Architecture. Available from: http://www.historynet.com/americas-greatest-work-architecture.htm [Accessed 02 October 2017].

13. O'dell, L. (1993) [Internet] Eichler Influenced by Wright: After Living in a House Designed by the Architect, Eichler Set Out to Build His Own and Never Quit. Available from: http://articles.latimes.com/1993-10-23/home/hm-48758_1_eichler-homes-building [Accessed 02 October 2017].

14. Isaacson, W. (2011). *Steve Jobs: The Exclusive Biography*. New York, Simon & Schuster, p. 7.

15. Blumenthal, K. (2012) *Steve Jobs: The Man Who Thought Different: A Biography*. New York, Feiwel and Friends.

16. Sheen, B. (2009) *Steve Jobs (People in the News)*. New York, Lucent Books.

17. Chouhan, S. (2011) [Internet] India visit gave a vision to Steve Jobs. Available from: http://indiatoday.intoday.in/story/india-visit-gave-a-vision-to-steve-jobs/1/154785.html [Accessed 02 October 2017].

18. Brennan, C. (2013) *The Bite in the Apple: A Memoir of My Life with Steve Jobs*. New York, St. Martin's Press.

19. ISAACSON, W. (2011) *Steve Jobs: The Exclusive Biography*. New York, Simon & Schuster, p. 359.

20. Stanford News (2005) [Internet] 'You've got to find what you love,' Jobs says. Available from: https://news.stanford.edu/2005/06/14/jobs-061505/ [Accessed 15 March 2017].

21. Fierstein, RK. (2015) [Internet] How the Inventor of the Polaroid Championed the Patent. Available from: https://www.theatlantic.com/technology/archive/2015/02/how-the-inventor-of-the-polaroid-saved-the-patent/385617/ [Accessed 15 March 2017].

22. First place belongs to the inventor of the light bulb, Thomas Edison, and his company.

23. Boston.com Staff (2012) [Internet] History of Polaroid and Edwin Land. Available from: https://www.boston.com/uncategorized/noprimarytagmatch/2012/10/03/history-of-polaroid-and-edwin-land [Accessed 15 March 2017].

24. The Economist (2015) [Internet] Land of hope and glory: The story of Polaroid. Available from: https://www.economist.com/news/books-and-arts/21647309-b ind-instant-photography-pioneer-there-stood-great-man-land-hope-and-glory?fsrc=rss [Accessed 15 March 2017].

The Dangers Of Entering Machine Age With An Anti-fluid Mind
The Ones Who Can Copy Better

1. Monegain, B. (2016) [Internet] IBM Watson accurately matches oncologists' advice, study finds. Available from: http://www.healthcareitnews.com/news/ibm-watson-accurately-matches-oncologists-advice-study-finds [Accessed 7 March 2017].

2. Lohr, S. (2017) [Internet] AI Is Doing Legal Work. But It Won't Replace Lawyers, Yet. *New York Times*. Available from: https://www.nytimes.com/2017/03/19/technology/lawyers-artificial-intelligence.html [Accessed 21 March 2017].

3. Frey, CB. & Osborne, MA. (2013) *The Future of Employment: How Susceptible are Jobs to Computerization?* Oxford Martin School, University of Oxford.

4. Nitto, H; Taniyama, D & Inagaki, H. (2017) [Internet] Social Acceptance and Impact of Robots and Artificial Intelligence—Findings of Survey in Japan, the US and Germany. Available from: https://www.nri.com/~/media/PDF/global/opinion/papers/2017/np2017211.pdf [Accessed 15 August 2017].

5. Mccurry, J. (2017) [Internet] Japanese company replaces office workers with artificial intelligence. Available from: https://www.theguardian.com/technology/2017/jan/05/japanese-company-replaces-office-workers-artificial-intelligence-ai-fukoku-mutual-life-insurance [Accessed 21 June 2017].

6. Peterson, H. (2016) [Internet] An unsettling new restaurant chain learns your preferences and serves your food with zero human interaction. Available from: http://www.businessinsider.in/An-unsettling-new-restaurant-chain-learns-your-preferences-and-serves-your-food-with-zero-humaninteraction/articleshow/51099575.cms [Accessed 15 March 2017].

7. Heath, T. (2016) [Internet] Bank tellers are the next blacksmiths. Available from: https://www.washingtonpost.com/business/economy/bank-tellers-are-the-next-blacksmiths/2017/02/08/fdf78618-ee1c-11e6-9662-6eedf1627882_story.html?utm_term=.05519953ad388 [Accessed 15 March 2017].

8. Boyd, J. (2016) [Internet] When machines can do any job, what will humans do? Available from: http://news.rice.edu/2016/02/14/when-machines-can-do-any-job-what-will-humans-do-2/ [Accessed 7 March 2017].

9. Johnston, C. (2016) [Internet] Artificial intelligence 'judge' developed by UCL computer scientists. Available from: https://www.theguardian.com/technology/2016/oct/24/artificial-intelligence-judge-university-college-london-computer-scientists [Accessed 21 March 2017].

10. Terdiman, D. (2016) [Internet] Inside the Hack Rod, The World's First AI-Designed Car. Available from: https://www.fastcompany.com/3054028/inside-the-hack-rod-the-worlds-first-ai-designed-car [Accessed 21 March 2017].

11. Source: http://censusindia.gov.in/Census_And_You/economic_activity.aspx

12. Editorial Team (2016) [Internet] The Future Has Arrived: World's First 3D Printed Office Is Inaugurated in Dubai. Available from: http://www.gensleron.com/work/2016/5/31/the-future-has-arrived-worlds-first-3d-printed-office-is-ina.html [Accessed 21 March 2017].

13. Fast Company (2016) [Internet] This Japanese Novel Authored by a Computer Is Scarily Well-Written. Available from: https://www.fastcompany.com/3058300/this-japanese-novel-authored-by-a-computer-is-scarily-well-written [Accessed 21 March 2017].

Yogini, Shakespeare, Mimicking And Machines

1. The facts on Madhusudan Gupta in this fictional story are indeed true. (source: Nath, SK. (2016) [Internet] First Human Dead Body Dissection in

the History of Medical Education in India & Pundit Madhusudan Goopta (1806-1856). Available from: http://www.aroiwb.org/ejournal/e-journal-jan-mar-2017/SankarNath.pdf [Accessed 5 April 2017].

Evolution Of A Rebellious Child

1. MD (Doctor of Medicine), in those days, was not a typical two-year postgraduate degree as it currently is in India. For instance, it took Robert Darwin only a few months to get his MD.

2. Dr Robert Darwin married Susannah, daughter of Josiah Wedgewood, one of the wealthiest industrialists of the world of the eighteenth century, which also contributed significantly to the wealth of the Darwin family.

3. Colp, R; Walton, M & Bell, W. (1982) Notes and Events. *Journal of the History of Medicine and Allied Sciences*. Vol. 37, no. 1, pp. 66–82.

4. Dr Robert Darwin also ran his medical practice from one of the wings of his residence.

5. People usually refer to Charles Darwin's birth house as 'The Mount' whereas it was the name of the place on a hill on which his father later built the house.

6. Taxidermy: the art of preparing, stuffing and mounting the skins of animals with lifelike effect.

7. Darwin, E. (1794) *Zoonomia; Or, the Laws of Organic Life*, Vol. I. Boston, D Carlisle.

8. Charles Darwin's theory of evolution by means of natural selection demonstrated that it is not necessarily the strongest species that survive but the fittest, which eventually is determined by random genetic variations transferred from one generation to the other, which specifically help the species to survive its environment.

9. The expression 'survival of the fittest' was coined by Herbert Spencer in *Principles of Biology* (1864), which he wrote after reading Charles Darwin's *On the Origin of Species*.

10. From Darwin's autobiography (p. 28): To my deep mortification my father once said to me, 'You care for nothing but shooting, dogs, and rat-catching, and you will be a disgrace to yourself and all your family.' Barlow, N. (ed) 1958. *The autobiography of Charles Darwin 1809-1882. With the original omissions restored. Edited and with appendix and notes by his grand-daughter Nora Barlow*. London, Collins.

11. Freethinkers are those who consider that facts and reasoning should be the foundation of reaching to truth rather than past beliefs, authority or dogmas.

12. Darwin, F. (ed) (1887) *The Life and Letters of Charles Darwin, Including an Autobiographical Chapter*. London, John Murray.

Lessons On Artificial Intelligence From A Nineteenth-century Storyteller

1. Titcomb, J. (2017) [Internet] AI is the biggest risk we face as a civilisation, Elon Musk says. Available from: http://www.telegraph.co.uk/technology/2017/07/17/ai-biggest-risk-face-civilisation-elon-musk-says/ [Accessed 5 September 2017].

2. Hall, G. (2017) [Internet] Zuckerberg blasts Musk warnings against artificial intelligence as 'pretty irresponsible'. Available from: https://www.bizjournals.com/sanjose/news/2017/07/24/elon-musk-artificial-intelligence-risk-zuckerberg.html [Accessed 5 September 2017].

3. Petroff, A. (2017) [Internet] Elon Musk says Mark Zuckerberg's understanding of AI is 'limited'. Available from: http://money.cnn.com/2017/07/25/technology/elon-musk-mark-zuckerberg-ai-artificial-intelligence/index.html [Accessed 5 September 2017].

4. Frey, CB. & Osborne, MA. (2013) The Future of Employment: How Susceptible are Jobs to Computerization? Oxford Martin School, University of Oxford.

5. Whether a job will be taken over by machines or be better done by a human is explained quite well by Noble laureate Herbert Simon in his paper, The Corporation: Will It Be Managed by Machines? In Anshen, ML & Bach, GL. (eds) (1985) *Management and the Corporations.* New York, McGraw-Hill, pp. 17–55.

6. Such doubts have already being expressed, for example as highlighted here: Naughton, J. (2017) [Internet] How a half-educated tech elite delivered us into chaos. Available from: https://www.theguardian.com/commentisfree/2017/nov/19/how-tech-leaders-delivered-us-into-evil-john-naughton [Accessed 20 November 2017].

7. Xinhua (2017) [Internet] AI to create over 100,000 jobs in one Chinese province alone. Available from: http://www.chinadaily.com.cn/china/2017-07/11/content_30064818.htm [Accessed 20 November 2017].

8. Knight, W. (2017) [Internet] Andrew Ng's Next Trick: Training a Million AI Experts. Available from: https://www.technologyreview.com/s/608573/andrew-ngs-next-trick-training-a-million-ai-experts/ [Accessed 8 August 2017].

9. Storing, searching and retrieving capabilities.

10. Hillis, K; Petit, M & Jarrett, K. (2013) *Google and the Culture of Search.* New York, Routledge, p. 209.

11. Moore, M. (2009) [Internet] HG Wells on Google: which of his predictions came true? Available from: http://www.telegraph.co.uk/technology/google/6218219/HG-Wells-on-Google-which-of-his-predictions-came-true.html [Accessed 8 August 2017].

12. Made with a budget of just over $90 million, *Hollow Man* made a profit of over $100 million.

13. Ahmed, S. (2015) [Internet] Was HG Wells the first to think of the atom bomb? Available from: http://www.bbc.com/news/magazine-33365776 [Accessed 8 August 2017].

14. The film *The War of the Worlds* was released in 2005 and grossed over $235 million.

15. Wells, HG. (1938) *World Brain*. London, Methuen & Co., Ltd.; Garden City, NY, Doubleday, Doran & Co., Inc.

16. Incidentally, while writing this account, the news came that the Madhya Pradesh government had banned sand mining from the banks of Narmada River. As Rahul's father, our fictional character, had exactly the same business, the move would have had substantial impact on his revenues. (Source: http://www.th indubusinessline.com/news/national/mp-govt-bans-sand-mining-in-narmada/article9709867.ece

But, I Am A Specialist, My Friend
The Pain Of A World-class Specialist

1. The Iraqi invasion of Kuwait on 2 August 1990 resulted in almost doubling of oil prices (increasing from $17 per barrel to $36 between July and October 1990) in a short span causing a brief recession and delaying key infrastructural activities worldwide.

2. Mukherjee, A. (2011) [Internet] 'Mass-Produced Engineers From Private Colleges With No Quality Are Of No Use To' [*sic*]. Available from: http://www.outlookindia.com/magazine/story/mass-produced-engineers-from-private-colleges-with-no-quality-are-of-no-use-to/277221[Accessed 8 August 2017].

3. Population Pyramid (2013) [Internet] India 1960. Available from: https://www.populationpyramid.net/india/1960/ [Accessed 5 May 2017].

4. Yathish, TR & Manula, CG. (2009) [Internet] How to Strengthen and Reform Indian Medical Education System: Is Nationalization the Only Answer? *Online Journal of Health and Allied Sciences*. Available from: http://cogprints.org/6968/1/2009-4-1.pdf [Accessed 5 May 2017].

5. In 2014 alone, the Bar Council of India approved 92 new law colleges, which means that every three days, one new law college was being approved.

6. Medical Council of India (2017) [Internet] List of Colleges Teaching MBBS. Available from: https://www.mciindia.org/ActivitiWebClient/informationdesk/listofCollegesTeachingMBBS [Accessed 5 November 2017].

7. Times Higher Education (2017) [Internet] World University Rankings 2018: Their dreams are not impossible. Available from: https://www.timeshighereducation.com/world-university-rankings-2018-their-dreams-are-not-impossible [Accessed 5 November 2017].

8. Mccarthy, N. (2017) [Internet] The Countries With The Most STEM Graduates [Infographic]. Available from: https://www.forbes.com/sites/niallmccarthy/2017/02/02/the-countries-with-the-most-stem-graduates-infographic/#5672c5ef268a [Accessed 5 November 2017].

9. Survey conducted by the Federation of Indian Chambers of Commerce and Industry (FICCI), an association of business organisations in India (Source: http://www.ficci.in/ficci-in-news-page.asp?nid=11962).

10. Mukherjee, A. (2011) [Internet] 'Mass-Produced Engineers From Private Colleges With No Quality Are Of No Use To' [sic]. Available from: http://www.outlookindia.com/magazine/story/mass-produced-engineers-from-private-colleges-with-no-quality-are-of-no-use-to/277221[Accessed 8 August 2017].

11. Ycharts (2017) [Internet] Infosys Market Cap: 36.01B for 7 December 2017. Available from: https://ycharts.com/companies/INFY/market_cap [Accessed 8 December 2017].

12. Infosys (2017) [Internet] Financials. Available from: https://www.infosys.com/investors/financials/Pages/employee-data.aspx [Accessed 8 December 2017].

13. PTI (2015) [Internet] No invention, earth-shaking idea from India in 60 years: Narayana Murthy. Available from: https://www.gadgetsnow.com/tech-news/No-invention-earth-shaking-idea-from-India-in-60-years-Narayana-Murthy/articleshow/48086325.cms [Accessed 8 December 2017].

The Sad Story Of A Brilliant Mind

1. Moore, M. (2015) [Internet] Goldman Investment Banker Gupta's Death Determined to Be Suicide. Available from: https://www.bloomberg.com/news/articles/2015-06-09/goldman-investment-banker-gupta-s-death-determined-to-be-suicide [Accessed 5 May 2017].

2. Roche, JL. (2015) [Internet] A Father's Heartbreaking Essay about the Untimely Death of His 22-year-old Goldman Sachs analyst son. Available from: http://www.businessinsider.in/A-fathers-heartbreaking-essay-about-the-untimely-death-of-his-22-year-old-Goldman-Sachs-analyst-son/articleshow/47518165.cms [Accessed 5 October 2017].

3. Wall Street Oasis (2015) [Internet] https://www.wallstreetoasis.com/forums/a-son-never-dies-by-sunil-gupta-moving-letter-from-a-father-of-an-ibanking-analyst [Accessed 5 October 2017].

4. Marlow, I. (2017) [Internet] Delhi pollution beats Beijing's as air quality goes off the chart. Available from: http://www.livemint.com/Politics/GKomAuLKoUJclYkQYaJumJ/Delhi-pollution-beats-Beijings-as-air-quality-goes-off-the.html [Accessed 10 November 2017].

5. Sharma, M. (2017) [Internet] As Delhi chokes on toxic air, masks, purifiers sale goes up. Available from: http://www.businesstoday.in/current/

economy-politics/as-delhi-chokes-on-toxic-air-purifiers-sale-goes-high/
story/263527.html [Accessed 10 November 2017].

6. The Hindu (2016) [Internet] India overtook China in number of deaths due
to pollution: Report. Available from: http://www.th indu.com/sci-tech/
energy-and-environment/India-overtook-China-in-number-of-deaths-due-
to-pollution-Report/article16643789.ece [Accessed 10 November 2017].

7. PTI (2015) [Internet] Living in Delhi like living in a gas chamber: HC.
Available from: https://timesofindia.indiatimes.com/city/delhi/Living-
in-Delhi-like-living-in-a-gas-chamber-HC/articleshow/50031355.cms
[Accessed 10 November 2017].

8. Prasad, R. (2017) [Internet] Most pollution-linked deaths occur in India.
Available from: http://www.th indu.com/sci-tech/energy-and-
environment/india-ranked-no-1-in-pollution-related-deaths-report/
article19887858.ece [Accessed 10 November 2017].

9. Kulkarni, P. (2017) [Internet] Sangli doctor's arrest unfolds a horrifying
tale of female foeticide racket covering Maharashtra, Karnataka. Available
from: http://www.firstpost.com/india/sangli-doctors-arrest-unfolds-a-
horrifying-tale-of-illegal-female-foeticide-racket-covering-maharashtra-
karnataka-3339986.html [Accessed 10 November 2017].

10. PTI (2017) [Internet] India likely to be third largest economy by 2028:
HSBC report. Available from: http://www.th indu.com/business/
Economy/india-likely-to-be-third-largest-economy-by-2028-hsbc-report/
article19703063.ece [Accessed 10 November 2017].

11. Sinha, P. (2017) [Internet] Fact-check: Did India fall 45 places in Global
Hunger Index rank from 2014 to 2017? Available from: http://www.
th indu.com/business/Economy/india-likely-to-be-third-largest-economy-
by-2028-hsbc-report/article19703063.ece [Accessed 10 November 2017].

The Fluid Specialists
'Be Water, My Friend'

1. It will not be an exaggeration to term *Vishnudharmottaram Puranam* as
the long lost ancient Indian text. I reached at this conclusion based on
the reactions I got when I initiated the topic with several historians,
commentators and public in general. This tempted me to go into greater
detail beyond what was required for *Fluid*. Initially, it seemed that there
had been only one complete English translation of the *Puranam* done by
great historian Stella Kramrisch published in 1928 by Calcutta University
Press (titled *The Vishnudharmottara*). *Vishnudharmottaram Puranam* consists of
three parts but only Part III (titled *A Treatise on Indian Painting and Image-
making*) was attempted by Kramrisch. However, Kramrisch's translation
does not contain the original *shloka*s. A much wider net revealed another
two translations by luminaries such as Priyabala Shah published in 1958

(titled *Shri Vishnudharmottara,* Ga wad's Oriental Series, CXXX) and C Sivaramamurti published in 1978 (titled *Chitrastra of the Vishnudharmottara,* Kanak Publication). Sivaramamurti's work carries Kramrisch's forward. Notably, none of these contain the original *shloka*s. I also noticed that almost all of the peer-reviewed articles on the *Puranam* were citing from these respective translations and not the original *shloka*s. I too initially extracted the data from the work of the three but wasn't happy with the absence of the original Sanskrit *shloka*s. This is when I decided to search for the original text. My initial efforts revealed that not very many local researchers are aware of this *puranam* and often confuse it with the much popular *Vishnu Puran*. In fact, a funny incident happened at the Delhi Book Fair, 2018. In my quest, I was frantically going from stall to stall including those dealing exclusively with Sanskrit and religious publications but with no success. On one of the stalls, a person in proper religious attire insisted that there is no such thing as *Vishnudharmottaram Puranam* and what I mean is the *Vishnu Puran*. My Delhi Book Fair exercise remained fruitless but eventually I found that there indeed has been a recent attempt to produce the original. In 2016, Chaukhamba Surbharati Prakashan, based in Varanasi, published the original along with the Hindi translation (titled *Vishnudharmottaramahapuranam*). What arrived in post were voluminous 2,000 pages spread over three giant books. The exhaustive translation is accomplished by Shivprasad Dvivedi. In the initial pages, virtuoso Dvivedi reveals that as a young man when he was once roaming through the streets of Gudri Bazaar, Varanasi, he spotted 'two very ancient copies' of *Vishnudharmottaram Puranam* and bought them for 1 rupee.

Dvivedi is convinced that *Vishnudharmottaram,* which consists of 17,000 *shloka*s is actually the annex of *Vishnu Puran* which contain 6,000 *shloka*s. *Vishnu Puran* is often referenced as a text with 23,000 *shloka*s and hence he concludes that the 'lost' 17,000 *shloka*s of *Vishnu Puran* are actually not lost but present in the form of *Vishnudharmottaram Puranam* (as also hinted, though not with as much conviction, at some places by Saha).

Dvivedi's translation also indicates that most of the citation available in public domain is using the secondary source of Kramrisch's translation and are in fact riddled with factual errors. For *Fluid,* I have relied on the original *shloka*s presented in Dvivedi's translation.

2. Socrates' style of transferring knowledge is termed the 'Socratic Method', under which knowledge is generated through arguments and counterarguments.

3. *Shloka*s are Sanskrit couplets, which are the key mode of communication in the ancient Indian texts.

4. *Chitra* stands for 'sketch' and *sutra* stands for 'principles'; thus, *Chitra sutra* may mean 'basic principles of sketching'.

5. '...for there is an upstart Crow, beautified with our feathers, that with his Tygers hart wrapt in a Players hyde, supposes he is as well able to bombast out a blanke verse as the best of you: and being an absolute Johannes fac totum, is in his owne conceit the onely Shake-scene in a countrey'. (Robert Greene, 1592, Groats-Worth of Witte, bought with a million of Repentance.

6. Born, H. (2012) Why Greene was Angry at Shakespeare. *Medieval & Renaissance Drama in England*. Vol. 25, pp. 133-173.

7. Guest, D. (1991). The hunt is on for the Renaissance Man of computing. *The Independent*, London.

8. PTI (2015) [Internet] PM Modi to unveil Rs 98,000 crore Smart City, Amrut projects on 25 June. Available from: http://indianexpress.com/article/ india/india-others/pm-modi-to-unveil-rs-98000-crore-smart-city-amrut-projects-on-june-25/ [Accessed 10 November 2017].

9. Geddes, P & Tyrwhitt, J. (1947) *Patrick Geddes in India*. London, L. Humphries.

10. Geddes, P. (1918) Town Planning Towards City Development: A Report to the Durbar of Indore. Indore, Holkar State Printing Press.

11. Meller, H. (1981) *Patrick Geddes 1854–1932*. London, The Architectural Press.

12. Holism as understood in ancient India simply meant that all beings—plants and animals and nature in general—share a unified relationship, and all forces impacting this relationship should be considered as the whole and not as parts.

13. Geddes, P. (1917) Town Planning in Kapurthala. A Report to HH the Maharaja of Kapurthala. Lucknow, Murray's London Printing Press.

14. This involves both receiving and contributing—he constantly works to strengthen the research base by contributing research to the field, through peer-reviewed, high-quality journals. Relevant research might include the impact of lifestyle, advancement in nutrition science, advancements in surgical procedures and discovery of new drugs.

15. e.g. contextual hereditary impact, genetic evolutionary history, molecular genetics, gene therapy.

16. e.g. gene therapy.

17. Whether such a cardiologist should work towards making health care accessible to the poor can be understood by our discussions in the next to next chapter.

The School That Produces The Highest Number Of Nobel Laureates

1. If one were to include those who initially had Indian citizenship, three more scholars—Har Gobind Khorana, Subramanyan Chandras har and Venkatraman Ramakrishnan—can be included in the list.

2. Chalfie, M. (2015) Forced Multidisciplinarity. Available from: http:// www.lindau-nobel.org/martin-chalfie-on-multidisciplinarity/ [Accessed September 2017].

3. ibid.

4. Moerner, WE. (2015) Thoughts on Multidisciplinarity. Available from: http://www.lindau-nobel.org/william-moerner-on-multidisciplinarity/ [Accessed September 2017].

5. Fröman, N. (1996) [Internet] Marie and Pierre Curie and the Discovery of Polonium and Radium. Available from: https://www.nobelprize.org/ nobel_prizes/themes/physics/curie/ [Accessed 12 July 2017].

6. APS NEWS (2004) [Internet] This Month in Physics History, December 1898: The Curies Discover Radium. *APS News*. Vol. 13, no. 11. Available from: https://www.aps.org/publications/apsnews/200412/history.cfm [Accessed 12 July 2017].

7. American Institute of Physics (2000) [Internet] The Nobel Prize and Its Aftermath. Available from: https://history.aip.org/exhibits/curie/recdis2. htm [Accessed 12 July 2017].

8. Woo, J. (1998) [Internet] A short history of the development of ultrasound in obstetrics and gynaecology. Available from: http://www.ob-ultrasound. net/history1.html [Accessed 12 July 2017].

9. Sen, A. (1990) More than 100 million women are missing. *New York Review of Books*. 20 December 1990, pp. 61–66.

10. In Amartya Sen's essay, India was not the only country to have 'missing women', hence the total number of 100 million (comprising of women who were not allowed to survive in parts of Asia, the Middle East and Northern Africa).

11. The Nobel Foundation (1998) [Internet] Amartya Sen—Biographical. Available from: http://www.nobelprize.org/nobel_prizes/ economicsciences/laureates/1998/sen-bio.html [Accessed 12 July 2017].

12. Dutta, K & Robinson, A. (1995). *Rabindranath Tagore: The Myriad-minded Man*. London, Bloomsbury, p. 205.

13. Pal, S. (2016) [Internet] #Travel Tales: Exploring Tagore's Santiniketan, an Abode of Learning Unlike Any in the World. Available from: https:// www.thebetterindia.com/66627/santiniketan-rabindranath-tagore-bengal/ [Accessed 22 October 2017].

14. Dutta, K & Robinson, A. (eds) (1997) *Selected Letters of Rabindranath Tagore*. Cambridge & New York, Cambridge University Press, p. 54.

15. Ghoshal, S. (2013) [Internet] Amartya Sen: The uncommon reader. Available from: http://www.livemint.com/Leisure/dYfK1J0BS3fDd92iF2OFuJ/ Amartya-Sen-The-uncommon-reader.html [Accessed 22 October 2017].

16. Sen, A. (2015) *The Country of First Boys and Other Essays*. New Delhi, *The Little Magazine* & Oxford University Press.

17. ibid.

18. ibid., p. xxvii.

19. ibid., p. xxix.

20. ibid.
21. ibid.
22. The Nobel Foundation (1998) [Internet] Amartya Sen—Biographical. Available from: http://www.nobelprize.org/nobel_prizes/economicsciences/laureates/1998/sen-bio.html [Accessed 12 July 2017].

The Bigger Fluid Questions
What Can We Learn From The Richest Man In The World And The Boy Who Broke The IIT-IIM Mould

1. Tenali Rama's real name was said to be Ramakrishna. He lost his father at a young age and hence shifted with his mother to his *mama*'s (mother's brother) house in a small town named Tenali, in the present state of Andhra Pradesh. As he spent his growing years in Tenali, he famously came to be known as Tenali Rama.
2. A title for those people who had large holdings of land on which they could collect rent (*lagaan* in local language) from landless farmers.
3. In Transparency International's Corruption Index, India ranked 79 in 2016, which means that there were 78 countries in the world that were less corrupt than India.
4. Nair, H. (2009) [Internet] Metro Man Sreedharan's pension tension. Available from: http://www.hindustantimes.com/india/metro-man-sreedharan-s-pension-tension/story-qqUoOScy1pwocjSeS7HwjO.html [Accessed 25 June 2017].
5. Barron, J. (2009) [Internet] Unnecessary Surgery. Available from: http://www.nytimes.com/1989/04/16/magazine/unnecessary-surgery.html?pagewanted=all [Accessed 03 September 2017].
6. A tube-shaped device of metal or plastic that is placed inside the blood-supplying arteries to improve blockage and prevent heart attacks.
7. LawRato (2016) [Internet] TBI Blogs: This Lawyer Is Responsible for Heart Stents Becoming Super Cheap in India. Available from: https://www.thebetterindia.com/91360/advocate-birendra-sangwan-reduce-price-heart-surgery/ [Accessed 03 September 2017].
8. Trivedi, I. (2017) [Internet] Govt Caps Prices of Coronary Stents in Huge Relief to Heart Patients. Available from: http://www.livemint.com/Science/l5e572cVeCWGCSRmvnTlqL/Coronary-stent-prices-slashed-by-up-to-400-in-huge-relief-t.html [Accessed 03 September 2017].
9. A simple explanation of an interpreter is provided in a three-minute YouTube video titled 'Interpreters and Compilers (Bits and Bytes, Episode 6)', which can be found at https://www.youtube.com/watch?v=_C5AHaS1mOA.
10. Gates, B. (1976) [Internet] Extract of Bill Gates' Open Letter to Hobbyists. Available from: http://www.digibarn.com/collections/newsletters/

homebrew/V2_01/gatesletter.html Homebrew Computer Club Newsletter Volume 2, Issue 1 [Accessed 02 August 2017].

11. Gates, B. (2012) [Internet] The Turning Point: Our First Trip to Africa. Available from: https://www.gatesnotes.com/About-Bill-Gates/The-Turning-Point-Our-First-Trip-to-Africa [Accessed 02 August 2017].

12. Bill and Melinda Gates Foundation (2017) [Internet] Foundation Factsheet. Available from: https://www.gatesfoundation.org/Who-We-Are/General-Information/Foundation-Factsheet [Accessed 02 August 2017].

13. Ni, P. (2007) [Internet] America's Least Philanthropic Companies. Available from: https://ssir.org/articles/entry/the_least_philanthropic_companies [Accessed 02 August 2017].

14. Carry, J & Martin, CE. (2011) [Internet] Apple's philanthropy needs a reboot. Available from: http://edition.cnn.com/2011/OPINION/09/03/martin.cary.apple.charity/index.html [Accessed 01 August 2017].

15. Neate, R. (2015) [Internet] Tim Cook plans to donate $800m fortune to charity before he dies. Available from: https://www.theguardian.com/technology/2015/mar/26/tim-cook-apple-donate-800m-fortune-charity [Accessed 01 August 2017].

16. Source: https://stanford.edu/~manup/Prakash-CV-Sept2014.pdf

17. Kormann, C. (2015) [Internet] Through the looking glass: Tim Cook plans to donate $800m fortune to charity before he dies. Available from: https://www.newyorker.com/magazine/2015/12/21/through-the-looking-glass-annals-of-science-carolyn-kormann [Accessed 01 August 2017].

18. Newby, K. (2012) [Internet] Prakash wins Gates grant for paper microscope development. Available from: https://med.stanford.edu/news/all-news/2012/11/prakash-wins-gates-grant-for-paper-microscope-development.html [Accessed 01 August 2017].

19. Patents by inventor Manu Prakash source: https://patents.justia.com/inventor/manu-prakash

20. Newby, K. (2017) [Internet] Inspired by a whirligig toy, Stanford bioengineers develop a 20-cent, hand-powered blood centrifuge. Available from: https://news.stanford.edu/2017/01/10/whirligig-toy-bioengineers-develop-20-cent-hand-powered-blood-centrifuge/ [Accessed 01 August 2017].

21. Source: http://bhamla.com/

22. Moerner, EW. (2015) Thoughts on Multidisciplinarity. Available from: http://www.lindau-nobel.org/william-moerner-on-multidisciplinarity/ [Accessed 03 September 2017].

The Power Of Combined Fluidity

1. A wide road with adjoining gardens running parallel, connecting the President's house and the India Gate, previously known as Kingsway.

2. Previous name of the Rajpath.

3. *On a side note*: How the Viceroy's House would appear from the Kingsway became the source of a major rift between good friends Lutyens and Baker. The Viceroy's House was planned to be on a hillock (Raisina Hill). The two blocks (North and South Block) were being designed by Baker alone. Lutyens initially agreed to let the blocks be built on the hillock and to position the Viceroy's house to the back. However, he soon realised his mistake, because as one approached the hill, the blocks would obstruct the view of Viceroy's House from the Kingsway due to its steep slope. He insisted that the bottom hill had to be dug up for an unobstructed view of the Viceroy's House, but Baker refused as the work had started. Lutyens could not get the decision to be reversed, and eventually ended his friendship with Baker. (Source: https://blogs.wsj.com/indiarealtime/2011/11/21/how-two-friends-built-a-city-and-fell-out/).

4. Hunt, T. (2014) *Cities of Empire. The British Colonies and the Creation of the Urban World*. Boston, Macmillan.

5. Bremner, GA. (2016) *Architecture and Urbanism in the British Empire*. Oxford, Oxford University Press.

6. Hunt, T. (2015) *Ten Cities that Made an Empire*. London, Penguin.

7. Translated as ten books on architecture.

8. Incidentally, when we see the Vitruvian Man, we assume it to be standing, however, as per the original explanation by Vitruvius, the man is lying on the floor with his face up.

9. While the facial expressions, gestures, hairstyle, etc. for sketching women are provided in detail, the women's measurements are not in much greater detail than that given here.

Image Credits

P. 8   *The Spinning Dancer* © Nobuyuki Kayahara, Source-Procreo Flash Design Laboratory. Under creative commons license. Source: https://commons.wikimedia.org/wiki/File:Spinning_Dancer.gif

P. 12   *The Apple Park: The flying-saucer-shaped recently opened headquarter of Apple Inc.* Photo by Carles Rabada on Unsplash

P. 32   *If you pull all the continents towards each other you will create Pangaea* © Ashish Jaiswal

P. 40   *Golden Horn Bridge design circa 1502* © Ashish Jaiswal/Under creative commons license. The single span bridge is redrawn from the original bridge design proposed by Leonardo da Vinci in 1502

P. 41   *Mona Lisa by architect/engineer Leonardo da Vinci* Under creative commons license. Source: https://www.pexels.com/photo/woman-art-painting-mona-lisa-40997/

P. 43   *Leonardo da Vinci's notebook with precise drawings of human foetus along with anatomical observations* Under creative commons license. Source: https://commons.wikimedia.org/wiki/File:Leonardo_da_Vinci_-_Studies_of_the_foetus_in_the_womb.jpg

P. 46   Under creative commons license. Source: https://commons.wikimedia.org/wiki/File:Newton-WilliamBlake.jpg

P. 56   *The ancient, two-sided Indian musical instrument, Mridanga* © Ashish Jaiswal

P. 58   *From a bamboo piece to a rudimentary flute* © Ashish Jaiswal

P. 59   *The finger movement to play harmonious tones (sur)* © Ashish Jaiswal

P. 61   *Transformation of mridanga into the tabla* © Ashish Jaiswal

P. 67   *Apple's net worth comparisons* © Ashish Jaiswal

P. 72   The geometric linearity introduced by Frank Lloyd Wright © Ashish Jaiswal/ Top image, Facade of a Victorian era house under creative commons license, source: https://images.metmuseum.org/CRDImages/dp/ original/DP803206.jpg/Fallingwater sketch under creative commons license/Joseph Eichler home style under creative commons license

P. 74   The transformation of Fröbel Gifts, Wright's architectural principles and Eichler's buildings into Apple products. © Ashish Jaiswal/The Apple Park Photo by Carles Rabada on Unsplash

P. 106   The Voyage of Charles Darwin 1831-1836 © Sémhur/Wikimedia Commons/ CC-BY-SA-3.0, or Free Art License

P. 106   Hourglass learning approach in the three generation of Darwins © Ashish Jaiswal

P. 115   Rudimentary Scale of Intelligence © Ashish Jaiswal

P. 130   The two-faced nature of the Indian education system © Ashish Jaiswal

P. 136   Growth of professional colleges in India © Ashish Jaiswal

P. 138   Growth of professional colleges in India © Ashish Jaiswal

P. 152   The interdisciplinary approach taught by Rishi Markandeya in Chitra Sutra, Vishnudharmottaram Puranam, chapter 2, shloka 1-9 © Ashish Jaiswal

P. 154   T-shaped model of specialisation (David Guest, 1991) © Ashish Jaiswal

P. 155   Fluid-wheel model of specialisation © Ashish Jaiswal

P. 158   The fluid-wheel of a smart-city specialist © Ashish Jaiswal

P. 160   The fluid-wheel of a cardiologist © Ashish Jaiswal

P. 174   Amartya Sen's fluid-wheel: The elements which shaped his thinking © Ashish Jaiswal

P. 185   An Open Letter to Hobbyists by Bill Gates Under creative commons license source: http://www.digibarn.com/collections/newsletters/homebrew/ V2_01/gatesletter.html

P. 186   Apple Inc's ad in 1976 in response to the open letter by Bill Gates © Apple Computer Company, Palo Alto, CA. Scanned from page 11 of the October 1976 Interface Age magazine by Michael Holley Swtpc6800. Under creative commons license

P. 189   Foldscope: a foldable microscope costing $1 (roughly 65 Indian rupees) invented by IITian Manu Prakash © Foldscope Instruments, Inc. 2018

P. 198   Combined intelligence journey of India Gate © Ashish Jaiswal

P. 199   India Gate: Elements inspired from Indian architecture Sanchi stupa under creative commons license source: John Marshall, 'A Guide to Sanchi', 1918 Plate II https://commons.wikimedia.org/wiki/File:Sanchi3.jpg

P. 201   Vitruvian Man by Leonardo da Vinci, created around 1490 under creative commons license source: https://commons.wikimedia.org/wiki/ File:Leonardo_da_Vinci-_Vitruvian_Man.JPG

P. 206   The Hans Man vs The Vitruvian Man © Ashish Jaiswal/The Vitruvian Man is redrawn from the original by Leonardo da Vinci under creative common license